YEAR 'ROUND ACTIVITIES
FOR TWO-YEAR-OLD
CHILDREN

Preschool Curriculum Activities Library

YEAR 'ROUND ACTIVITIES FOR TWO-YEAR-OLD CHILDREN

Anthony J. Coletta, Ph.D.

Associate Professor of Early Childhood Education
William Paterson College, Wayne, New Jersey

Kathleen Coletta

Illustrated by Margie Tuohy Jordan

THE CENTER FOR APPLIED RESEARCH IN EDUCATION INC., WEST NYACK, NEW YORK

Fifth Printing . . . . . July 1987

*To our sons, Michael and Daniel,
who make every day a challenge,
a wonder, and a joy*

Library of Congress Cataloging-in-Publication Data

Coletta, Anthony J.
    Year 'round activities for two-year-old children.

    (Preschool curriculum activities library)
    Includes bibliographical references.
    1. Education, Preschool—Curricula—Handbooks
manuals, etc.   2. Perceptual-motor learning—Handbooks,
manuals, etc.   3. Play—Handbooks, manuals, etc.
4. Creative activities and seat work—Handbooks,
manuals, etc.   I. Coletta, Kathleen. II. Title.
III. Series: Coletta, Anthony J. Preschool curriculum
activities library.
LB1140.4.C64   1986   372.19   85-24264

ISBN 0-87628-981-2

Printed in the United States of America

ABOUT THE AUTHORS

Anthony J. Coletta, Ph.D., is presently associate professor of Early Childhood Education at William Paterson College (Wayne, New Jersey), where he teaches Early Childhood Education courses. The holder of a Montessori teaching certificate, Dr. Coletta has taught at all levels, preschool to junior high, working with both gifted and learning disabled preschool and primary children.

Kathleen Coletta, B.A., Early Childhood Education, is an experienced preschool teacher and currently serves as the Director of the Ponds Valley Preschool in Oakland, New Jersey. She has also served as a consultant to other area preschools developing curriculum manuals, newsletters, and a parent-education program.

ACKNOWLEDGMENTS

We thank ...

... **Margie Tuohy Jordan** for painstakingly reviewing each activity so that our ideas could be accurately depicted in her drawings. We also appreciate her creative suggestions.

... **Michelle Lyons** for typing all three manuscripts with accuracy, efficiency, and patience.

... **Donna Reid and the staff** of the Donna Reid Child Development Center, Franklin Lakes, New Jersey, for encouraging and implementing our curriculum plan as it was developed and giving us continuous feedback, criticisms, and suggestions. The teachers who cooperated during the field testing were Kathy Tenkate, Linda Fitzsimmons, Lois Wallace, Lori Doda, Rose Silvestri, and Emily Lio.

... **Bob Messano** for his original songs.

.. **John Sheehan and Kevin DeFreest** for their musical arrangements.

... **Faith Geruldsen, LeAnn Bucco, and Dawn Ciarleglio,** graduate students at William Paterson College, Wayne, New Jersey, for assisting with the research of books, fingerplays, records, and poetry that enhanced our curriculum and for contributing their own teaching ideas.

... **William Strader,** doctoral candidate in early childhood education at the University of Massachusetts, Amherst, Massachusetts, for contributing many suggestions based on his extensive experience as a preschool teacher and director.

... **Alpha Caliandro,** associate professor of early childhood education at William Paterson College, for guiding our selections of classical music pieces recommended in the activities.

... **Dr. Laura Aitken, Dr. Marge Moreno, and Joan Heins,** faculty of Early Childhood Education at William Paterson College, for their astute observations and recommendations regarding parts of the manuscript.

We further wish to acknowledge those traditional nursery rhymes, action songs, and fingerplays for which no authors have been located and that appear in many other books.

CHARACTERISTICS OF TWO-YEAR-OLD CHILDREN

The second year of life is a time of rapid overall growth. As the Skills-Concepts Checklist shows, early two-year-olds may speak in sentences of three or more words and correctly use approximately 50 words, while at age three, children use longer sentences and their vocabulary may consist of nearly 900 words.*

Like all preschool children, two-year-olds are egocentric; that is, they are unable to see another's point of view and therefore find it difficult to share materials and toys. This is particularly true of later two-year-olds and early three-year-olds, who often demonstrate resistant behavior around transition times.

Nevertheless, two-year-olds *are* capable of demonstrating certain skills, and the activities in this book support those abilities. For example, two-year-olds are beginning to enjoy looking at books and listening to stories. They can imitate the behavior of other children as well as the actions of an adult. In art, they are able to paste collage pieces to paper. Further, their vertical scribbling strokes eventually evolve into faces as they approach the age of three.

Two-year-olds' play is primarily sensory-motor, which is the free movement of large and small muscles. They are able to walk up and down stairs and run without constantly falling. Late two-year-olds can engage in simple symbolic or make-believe play. They can pretend to drink from a cup, for example, by using a cylindrical block instead of a real cup.**

These and many other characteristics are classified under the areas of cognitive, language, self, social studies, math, science, and gross and fine motor movements, and are listed in the Skills-Concepts Checklist for Two-Year-Olds. These seventy-two skills and concepts are sequentially presented and systematically developed in the children through carefully planned activities for September through June.

Using this book will save you considerable time that would normally be allotted to short- and long-term curriculum planning. More important, the time you spend teaching children will be used more effectively. Please refer to the following section for specific suggestions for using this book, the Checklist, and the activities.

* Margaret Lay-Dopyera and John Dopyera, *Becoming a Teacher of Young Children*, 2nd ed. (Lexington, Mass.: Heath, 1982).

** Charles F. Wolfgang, *Growing and Learning Through Play* (New York: McGraw-Hill, 1981).

SKILLS-CONCEPTS CHECKLIST*
FOR TWO-YEAR-OLDS
(Developmental Characteristics)

A child who is 24 to 36 months of age tends to develop skills rapidly. The following abilities will emerge as the child approaches age three. The activities within this book have been designed to develop the skills and concepts listed below in a manner consistent with the child's needs and interests. Monitor the child's progress and evaluate it twice during the school year by placing a check (√) next to the skill or concept once it has been mastered.

Name _____ Birthdate _____

COGNITIVE

Personal Curiosity/Autonomy	JAN.	JUNE
1. Shows curiosity and interest in surroundings		
2. Imitates the actions of adults		
3. Imitates play of other children		
4. Finds own play area or activity		
5. Enjoys looking at books		
6. Begins to notice differences between safe and unsafe environments (2½ to 3)		

Senses		
7. Begins to develop senses of touch, smell, taste, and hearing		
8. Begins to place large puzzle pieces in appropriate slots		

Memory		
9. Refers to self by name		
10. Points to common object on command		
11. Associates use with common objects		
12. Stacks three rings by size		
13. Knows that different activities go on at different times of the day (2½ to 3)		
14. Understands the idea of waiting for someone else to go first (2½ to 3)		

Creativity		
15. Shows simple symbolic play (pretends block is a cup)		
16. Acts out a simple story (2½ to 3)		
17. Draws a face (no arms or legs) (2½ to 3)		

Comments:

_____

_____

_____

* This Checklist was developed from the *Skill-Concept Development Checklists for Two Through Five Year Olds* (St. Louis County, Missouri: Parent-Child Early Education). Developed by the Ferguson-Florissant School District. Parts reprinted with their permission.

LANGUAGE

Sentence Structure	JAN.	JUNE
18. Describes what happened in two or three words		
19. Verbalizes wants ("Want water.")		
20. Repeats parts of songs, rhymes, and fingerplays		
21. Gives first and last names when asked (2½ to 3)		
22. Uses short sentences to convey simple ideas (2½ to 3)		

Listening

	JAN.	JUNE
23. Listens to simple stories and songs		
24. Follows simple directions		
25. Places objects in, on, beside, or under		
26. Identifies loud and soft		

Labeling

	JAN.	JUNE
27. Identifies own gender		
28. Identifies boy or girl		
29. Identifies self in mirror		
30. Names common objects in pictures		

Comments:

_____

_____

_____

_____

_____

SELF

	JAN.	JUNE
31. Points to six body parts when named		
32. Puts on and removes coat unassisted		
33. Lifts and drinks from cup and replaces on table		
34. Spoon feeds without spilling		
35. Begins to understand cleanliness		
36. Helps put things away		

Comments:

_____

_____

_____

SOCIAL STUDIES

	JAN.	JUNE
37. Identifies self from a snapshot		
38. Shows pleasure in dealing with people and things		
39. Values own property and names personal belongings (2½ to 3)		
40. Follows simple rules in a game run by an adult (2½ to 3)		

Comments:

_____

_____

_____

_____

MATH

Counting

	JAN.	JUNE
41. Understands the concept of "one"		
42. Counts two (repeats two digits)		
43. Indicates awareness of more than two (2½ to 3)		

Classifying

44. Groups things together by size (one category) (2½ to 3)		

Size Differences

45. Points to big and little objects (2½ to 3)		

Shapes

46. Differentiates circle and square (2½ to 3)		

Comments:

_____

_____

_____

_____

SCIENCE (2½ to 3)

Concepts

47. Knows the names of three animals		
48. Can associate the words *grass, plants,* and *trees* with correct objects		
49. Identifies rain, clouds, and sun		
50. Begins to understand hard and soft		
51. Begins to understand hot and cold		
52. Begins to understand wet and dry		
53. Matches two color samples		

Comments:

_____

_____

_____

GROSS MOTOR

Arm-Eye Coordination

54. Throws a small object two feet		
55. Catches a rolled ball and rolls it forward		

Body Coordination

56. Jumps with two feet		
57. Claps with music		
58. Walks on tip toe		
59. Walks upstairs alone (both feet on each step) (2½ to 3)		
60. Walks downstairs alone (both feet on each step) (2½ to 3)		
61. Hops on one foot (2½ to 3)		

Comments:

_____

_____

_____

FINE MOTOR

Finger Strength and Dexterity	**JAN.**	**JUNE**
62. Fills and dumps containers with sand		
63. Turns single pages (2½ to 3)		

Eye-Hand Coordination

64. Applies glue and pastes collage pieces		
65. Paints with a large brush		
66. Tears paper		
67. Strings five large beads		
68. Colors with a large crayon		
69. Rolls, pounds, and squeezes clay		
70. Draws a horizontal line		
71. Builds a six-block tower (2½ to 3)		
72. Uses scissors with one hand to cut paper (2½ to 3)		

Comments: _____

_____

_____

_____

ABOUT THE
PRESCHOOL CURRICULUM ACTIVITIES LIBRARY

Year 'Round Activities for Two-Year-Old Children is the first volume of three in the *Preschool Curriculum Activities Library*. This *Library* represents a multisensory developmental approach to curriculum development for two-, three-, and four-year-old children. The activities presented stimulate the senses of sight, touch, hearing, smell, and taste, while being appropriate to the children's stages of development. Several important research models provide a foundation for creative lesson plans that help you solve the major organizational problem in early childhood education—matching developmentally appropriate daily activities to traditional preschool topics.

In this *Library,* the major work of building a preschool curriculum has been done for you. Topics, skills, and concepts that have been "matched" to the proper stage of the child's growth are included in all the activities. Topics in the form of themes and subthemes have been carefully identified and ordered and are based on seasonal interest. A total of 585 activities are described in the three-book *Library,* and each one is based on skills identified in the Checklists for two-, three-, and four-year-old children.

More important, each book of the *Preschool Curriculum Activities Library* has been field tested to provide you with a complete developmental program. In addition, **Developmental Skills-Concepts Checklists*** are included for this age group as well as the other two age groups in the *Library*. (See the Complete Preschool Development Plan at the back of the book.) Each Checklist is an individual skills record that outlines the abilities you can reasonably expect from children at each age.

The following uses are recommended for the preceding Skills-Concepts Checklist for Two-Year-Olds found on pages viii-xi:

- Assess a child's skill and concept ability levels. This information of children's strengths and/or deficiencies can help modify curriculum plans by creating or changing activities.

- Monitor a child's progress throughout the year. Duplicate the Checklist for each child and keep it in his or her folder. Supplement the Checklist evaluations with anecdotal statements. It is recommended that the Checklist be completed twice yearly, in January and June.

- Use the Checklist as a progress report to parents and as a reference during parent conferences. Specific statements rather than broad generalizations can be made. Parents who are concerned about skill-concept development will be assured that their children will not miss any major topics, concepts, or skills.

- Use to individualize instruction by grouping children with a common strength or weakness. Teaching one lesson to a small group needing similar skill development saves the teacher's time and energy.

- Give the Checklist to the child's teacher next year. He or she will then know what skills the child has been exposed to and can more easily plan reinforcement and extension.

*The Skills-Concepts Checklist was originally developed by Dr. Walter Hodges of Georgia State University, Atlanta, Georgia, while he was working as a consultant with the Ferguson-Florissant schools in Ferguson, Missouri. The Checklist has been further modified by the authors to include the findings of other early childhood authorities, notably Dr. Carol Seefeldt, *A Curriculum for Preschools,* 2nd ed. (Columbus, O.: Chas. E. Merrill, 1980); Dr. Joseph Sparling, *Learningames for the First Three Years* (New York: Walker and Co., 1979); and Dr. Charles F. Wolfgang, *Growing and Learning Through Play* (New York: McGraw-Hill, 1981).

- Use the Checklist to understand the total development of children as they pass through the preschool years. The Checklist can also be used for inservice training, parent workshops, or orienting new staff members.
- Use a checkmark (√) to keep track of those skills mastered by the children. With this simple checking system, you can quickly scan the Checklist, noting the skills and concepts required. These skills and concepts can be reinforced as part of routine activities as you desire.

Each skill or concept has been carefully integrated into the curriculum. You know that the differences among two-, three-, and four-year-olds are more impressive than among seven-, eight-, and nine-year-olds. The Checklist provides a justification for creating differentiated learning experiences with classes of two-, three-, and four-year-olds. It can easily be reproduced for use in individual record keeping, as a progress report to parents, and as a tool for individualizing instruction.

Monthly themes and weekly subthemes of high interest are included as part of a unit approach to curriculum development. Within the unit framework, an entire preschool can study a broad topic for one month, separated into four related areas or weekly subthemes. The five activities within each subtheme are organized to develop and reinforce the skills and concepts found on the Skills-Concepts Checklist.

The ten themes and thirty-nine subthemes, one for each month and week of the school year, were created with the following concepts in mind:

1. Learning begins with the selection of topics that are most familiar to children and gradually expands into areas that are more challenging.
2. Good teaching involves creative long- and short-range planning. Within a well-organized framework, teachers can follow the child's lead and expand on his or her interests.
3. A thematic approach to curriculum development is most effective when the themes are highly related to the immediate environment surrounding the child.

Every effort has been made to connect topics to the seasonal events children will see and hear about each month. While this is not a holiday curriculum, some holidays are included in the subthemes and activities. For example, the November theme, "Home and Family," is strongly related to the meaning of Thanksgiving. Religious holidays, however, are not included within the themes and subthemes. Such holidays should be observed by each school in a manner appropriate to local cultural traditions.

195 ready-to-use activities are described for an entire school year of thirty-nine weeks (or ten months). Along with a multisensory emphasis, many physical movement suggestions are included to help children explore each topic as an active participant, at his or her own pace.

The activities can be used either with a whole group or in small groups. Whenever possible, you should aim to accomplish the activities in small groups or individually. Each activity, one for each day of the school year, includes the skill or concept to be learned, behavioral objectives, materials needed, a step-by-step procedure, and ways to vary or extend the activity.

Each of the thirty-nine subthemes contains five activities selected from the subject areas described here. Read the activities before trying them, so that materials such as books, records, posters, puzzles, and other recommended resources can be located or ordered, and the activities can be modified to best meet the needs of the children you teach.

By using these activities as a springboard, you can create challenging and involving activities that can be easily integrated into any existing educational framework.

The following subject areas are covered in the *Preschool Curriculum Activities Library*:

Language Arts. The language arts activities in this curriculum follow a language experience approach. The children's receptive and expressive language is enhanced through the use of fingerplays, nursery rhymes, poetry, discussions, and experience charts. Furthermore, many fine books for children are suggested, including Caldecott Medal and Honor books.

There are no formal reading or writing experiences among the 195 activities. Such experiences are appropriate for the concrete stage of development, ages seven to eleven. Stimulating experiences, along with the manipulation of objects, are much more important for preschoolers than ditto sheets and workbook activities.

Science. The science activities are aimed at encouraging observation, comparison, exploration, testing, inquiry, and problem solving. Within many activities, children's senses are stimulated. You can help them notice cause and effect, as well as keep simple records.

Nutrition/Foods Experience. With the nutrition activities, children learn about group cooperation, weights and measures, time, and changes of matter from one form to another. Moreover, they develop an understanding of how to follow directions in sequence, gain pleasure from creating simple foods, and develop good eating habits.

Creative Dramatics/Movement. Creative dramatics aid children in developing language and spontaneous play. Creative dramatics can take many forms, such as creative movement (in which children use sensory-motor abilities and gain skill in body control), rhythm, tempo, timing, following directions, and group cooperation. While involved in creative dramatics, children sometimes use concrete objects as symbols, and you can extend their play to include pantomime, story dramatizations, role playing, and puppetry.

Social Studies. The social studies activities focus on learning about self, home, family, transportation, and the immediate as well as the larger community. Emphasis is on the children's involvement in their own learning. Therefore, field trips to local sites are an important part of the curriculum. The Variations/Ways to Extend sections of several lessons suggest inviting parents and other community people into the classroom to share their special talents and information.

Art. Art for preschoolers is a creative process that allows for choice, exploration, and imaginative expression in a pleasant, supportive atmosphere. Each child's work should be unique and recognizably different from another's. These process goals are best reached through traditional preschool techniques such as painting at an easel, finger painting, and rolling and molding clay.

The art experiences suggested in the *Library* are tied to particular curriculum topics. In this sense, the art activities are limited in their potential for pure, creative experience because they have been suggested as ways to reinforce certain ideas for the children. Keeping in mind that any activity described in this book is meant to be only *one* experience in a whole week of related activities, you must be certain to provide the children with plenty of pure art activities at other times. Opportunities for exploring color, line, and form and for discovering the effects of various media on different surfaces in an open-ended fashion will allow each child to make a personal statement with art.

Exposure to beautiful works of art can enhance the classroom environment. A number of activities include suggestions for obtaining inexpensive color reproductions from the National Gallery of Art. These have special appeal for young children, such as the work of Renoir and Matisse.

Music. The goals of the music experiences are to develop appreciation, participation, and responsiveness; musical competencies such as listening, performance, rhythm, and creativity; and musical concepts such as pitch, volume, and contrasts. Many recorded songs are suggested along with new original music specifically designed for this curriculum. In addition, certain classical pieces that provide stimulating background music and exposure to the works of great composers are recommended.

Math. The math activities attempt to reflect the needs of the preoperational child, ages two to seven. Opportunities are presented that allow children to learn through direct experiences such as sorting, comparing, and ordering. Playful lessons develop skills in rote counting, numeral recognition, and sets. Again, duplicated sheets are not utilized in any of the math activities because they are a semiconcrete rather than a concrete vehicle for learning.

Thinking and Gross Motor Games. The thinking games motivate children to develop cognitive skills within a play situation. When involved in a thinking game, children are learning to identify, classify, and apply skills.

Gross motor games contribute to positive physical and mental health by strengthening muscles and helping to free children from tension. Social development is aided when the children cooperate and learn the positions of leader and follower. Finally, self-concepts are enhanced as youngsters acquire motor skills and feelings of success and enjoyment.

A Complete Preschool Development Plan consisting of the three Checklists is included at the end of each book. This Plan displays the developmental skills progression for two-, three-, and four-year-olds, giving you a clear picture of the prekindergarten skills children can be expected to develop. While educators know that learning is uneven (that is, a child who is three may not necessarily demonstrate all the three-year-old skills), the Plan gives you an overall idea of how normal development progresses and a place to start in assessing children's development. It also serves as a visual presentation of the cognitive theory that ideas grow from concrete to abstract and from simple to complex as the child learns and grows.

The three books in the *Library* can be used independently or simultaneously by a school that has classes for two-, three-, and four-year-olds. The children can study the same topics but in ways that are of interest to and appropriate for their level of growth. This exciting concept can mobilize a school and encourage total involvement of students, teachers, and parents in learning—all working together to help the children develop and grow to their fullest potential.

Anthony J. Coletta
Kathleen Coletta

CONTENTS

Police Officers and Firefighters

Shopkeepers and Office Workers

Librarians and Postal Workers

The Ocean, Rivers, and Lakes

Insects

LEARNING ABOUT OURSELVES AND OTHERS

○ Getting to Know One Another

○ Self-Concept

○ Friends and School

Weekly Subtheme: Getting to Know One Another

I-1 MY LETTER

Subject Area: Art

Concepts/Skills: Explores a medium
Applies paste and glues paper
Follows directions

Objectives: The children will participate in a rhyme that helps them to identify classmates and will create a collage based on an initial.

Materials:
- Words to fingerplay (see Procedures section)
- Precut block letter initial for each child
- Paste
- Collage paper
- Construction paper

Procedure:

1. Say the following fingerplay to the children, using two names from the group each time (for example, Elaine and Phil), as a way of familiarizing them with one another:

   Two little children
   Sitting in a room.
   One named *Elaine*
   The other named *Phil.*
   Run away *Elaine*,
   Run away *Phil.*
   Come back *Elaine*,
   Come back *Phil.*

   Children can run away from the circle when they hear that part, and then return. Repeat for each pair of children.

2. Give each child a large block letter that is his or her first initial. Hand out all the *A*'s at one time, then all the *B*'s, and so forth to provide reinforcement. Show the children how to apply paste to the back of the letters and glue them onto construction paper. Provide them with lots of cut-up colored paper to collage right on their initials.

Variations/Ways to Extend:

- Instead of making a collage of their first initial, give the children watercolor paints and brushes to paint their letters.
- Hold up a completed initial collage and say, "This is an *A*. Who has another *A* collage to show us now?"
- Read *The First Words Picture Book* by Bill Gillham (New York: Putnam Publishing Group, 1982).

I-2   WHAT'S YOUR NAME?

Subject Area: Music

Concepts/Skills: Repeats parts of rhymes
Listens to simple songs

Objectives: The children will learn a new song that helps introduce them to one another.

Material: • Music or tune to "Row, Row, Row Your Boat"

Procedure:

1. Sing the following verse to the tune of "Row, Row, Row Your Boat":

   Who, who, who are you?
   It would be so fine
   If you tell me what your name is
   I will tell you mine.

2. Sit the children in a semicircle in front of you. Sing the song through a few times using another teacher or an outgoing, verbal child as a partner. Have the children join in singing the song with you.

Variation/Way to Extend:

• Use this song as part of opening circle activities, with you singing to each child.

I–3   THIS IS OUR ROOM

Subject Area: Social Studies

Concept/Skill: Finds own play area or activity

Objectives: The children will be introduced to the learning areas around the room and will be able to find a play area or activity.

Material: • Learning areas or centers

Procedure:

1. Arrange the room into appropriate learning areas for two-year-olds. Carefully select equipment and materials that provide a safe, stimulating environment in which autonomy, gross motor skills, and intellectual development are all encouraged. Some suggestions include a block area; an art center; a manipulative table with beads for stringing, objects to sort, puzzles to put together, and toys that snap, twist, and turn; an indoor gross motor center in which children can sit on wheel toys, throw and catch large balls, or climb through plastic tunnels; sand and water tables with pouring, scooping, and straining items; and a science table with real objects for the children to explore.

2. Show each individual child the areas so that each child can select what interests him or her most throughout the day.

Variation/Way to Extend:

• Color-code many materials to a place on a shelf so that the children will gain a measure of autonomy by being able to put away their own play objects.

Weekly Subtheme: Getting to Know One Another

I–4 WHAT DO I LOOK LIKE?

Subject Area: Language Arts

Concept/Skill: Identifies self in mirror

Objectives: The children will use hand mirrors to recognize themselves and to express emotions.

Material: • Hand mirror

Procedure:

1. This first week in preschool is likely to be an emotional one for two-year-olds. Giving them an opportunity to look at themselves in a mirror and recognize themselves can add to their self-confidence. Use a hand mirror for each child or hang a mirror in the room at the children's eye level.

2. Talk to the children about who they see in the mirror and how he or she looks—happy or sad. Talk about looking happy, about all the reasons for being happy to be in a preschool, and about all the fun things you will be doing together.

Variations/Ways to Extend:

- Sit the children in a circle and sing "Here We Are Together" to the tune of "Did You Ever See a Lassie?":

  Here we are together, together, together
  Here we are together, all here on the floor.
  There's (name of child) and (name of child)
  [point to each child and say his or her name]
  And (name of child) and (name of child).
  Here we are together, all here on the floor.

- Encourage the children to clap hands together as they sing the song.

Weekly Subtheme: Getting to Know One Another

I–5 WHO'S MISSING?

Subject Area: Thinking Games

Concepts/Skills: Follows simple directions
Imitates play of other children
Places objects in, on, beside, and under

Objectives: The children will participate in a game and recall who their classmates are.

Material: • Objects large enough to hide behind or under

Procedure:

1. Explain to the class that they are going to play a hide-and-seek game called "Who's Missing?"

2. Select a child who is to be "it." Show him or her and the class several places in the room in which one could hide. Ask the child to cover his or her eyes. Select another child in the class to hide in one of the designated places. When the child is safely hidden, ask the child who is "it" to look and guess "Who's Missing." You may give hints or rename all the children who are in the class. When he or she names the missing child, have them tell where they think the child is hiding, for instance, under the table, behind the door. When the child correctly answers, have him or her pick another classmate by name to be "it" and play again.

Variation/Way to Extend:

• Decorate a small cardboard box and gather a few small toys. Further demonstrate that concepts of "in," "on," "beside," and "under" by placing the toys appropriately in relation to the box.

Weekly Subtheme: Self-Concept

I–6   PAT-A-CAKE

Subject Area: Music

Concepts/Skills: Is self-aware
Follows directions
Appreciates and participates

Objectives: The children will learn a nursery rhyme and listen for their names to be sung.

Material: • Words to "Pat-a-Cake"

Procedure:

1. Teach the children the old English nursery rhyme:

    Pat-a-cake, Pat-a-cake, baker's man,
    Bake me a cake as fast as you can.
    Pat it and shape it and mark it with a <u>B</u>,
    And bake it in the oven for <u>Baby</u> and me.

2. Sing the rhyme several times, each time substituting the first letter of a child's name for the "B" and the name itself for "Baby." For example,

    "... and mark it with a C,
    And bake it in the oven for Chuckie and me."

3. Do this for all children in the group and tell them to listen for their names. They may stand when they hear their own name called.

Variations/Ways to Extend:

• Sing the first three lines of the rhyme slowly, and the last one quickly to demonstrate the contrast of fast and slow to the children.
• Give the children toy telephones or contact the educational office of your telephone company to borrow some real phones to let the children have fun practicing saying their names.
• Play some songs from the album *Music for Ones and Twos* by Tom Glazer (CMS Records, 14 Warren Street, New York, N.Y. 10017).

Weekly Subtheme: Self-Concept

I-7 COLLAGE OF COLOR

Subject Area: Art

Concepts/Skills: Explores creatively
Applies glue and pastes collage pieces
Is aware of printed names

Objective: The children will create their own collages.

Materials:
- Colored tissue paper
- Construction paper
- Scissors
- School glue
- Glue brushes
- Containers of water

Procedure:

1. Prepare the tissue paper in advance by cutting it into various shapes. Prepare the glue by diluting it with water in the containers to a thin consistency.
2. Let the children work individually or in small groups. Tell them that they are going to make their own pictures. Give each child a sheet of construction paper, some tissue shapes, and a container of glue with a brush. Let each child brush glue where desired on the paper and then attach the tissue shape.
3. Encourage students to fill the space in whatever way they like and to experiment with thicker areas where the tissue has been layered.
4. When dry, label each picture with the child's name. Show the child what you are doing and what the letters mean.

Variations/Ways to Extend:

- Prepare containers with a variety of materials (felt, fabrics, feathers, styrofoam pieces, and so forth) for other types of collages to be made at other times.
- Let the children work on a group collage as an ongoing project. Attach a large sheet of kraft paper to a wall and let the children take it down and work on it periodically or when they want to.

I-8 DRESS UP DAN OR DAWN

Subject Area: Social Studies

Concepts/Skills: Identifies boy or girl
Points to common object on command
Associates use with common objects

Objectives: The children will identify and discuss clothing.

Materials:
- Pictures of children in basic clothes cut from mail-order catalogs and mounted on light cardboard or construction paper
- Large flannelboard
- Large doll shape (see the pattern on the next page) cut from tan or neutral felt
- Clothes items cut from colored felt to fit felt doll (boy clothes for Dan, girl clothes for Dawn)

Procedure:

1. Ask the children questions about what they are wearing to school.
2. Show the mounted picture and ask each child to point out a particular article of clothing. Ask them where it is worn—on the head, feet, and so forth.
3. Introduce dressed-up felt doll Dan or Dawn.
4. Ask the children questions about what the doll is wearing.
5. Remove the clothes from the doll and let the children take turns getting him or her dressed for school. Talk about whether it is a warm or cold, sunny or rainy day. Ask the children to name the articles of clothing and where they are going to place them on Dan or Dawn. Help the children put clothes on in the proper order, that is, underwear first.

Variations/Ways to Extend:

- Each day as part of opening circle routine have the children discuss the weather and dress Dawn or Dan to come to school appropriately, using, for example, an umbrella, snow boots, and so forth.
- Let the children practice putting on coats and removing them unassisted.
- Listen to Hap Palmer's record of "What Are You Wearing?" (Educational Activities, Inc., P.O. Box 392, Freeport, N.Y. 11520).

Weekly Subtheme: Self-Concept

I-9 OPEN, SHUT THEM

Subject Area: Language Arts

Concepts/Skills: Points to six body parts when named
Repeats parts of a rhyme

Objective: The children will recall the words to a new fingerplay.

Material: • Words to the fingerplay (see Procedure section)

Procedure:

1. Ask the children to sit in a semicircle on the floor or in chairs so everyone can see.

2. Demonstrate the motions as you say the following fingerplay:

> Open, shut them;
> Open, shut them;
> Give your hands a clap!
> Open, shut them;
> Open, shut them;
> Lay them in your lap.
> Creepy, creep them;
> Creepy, creep them;
> Right up to your chin.
> Open up your little mouth,
> But do not let them in!

3. Repeat the fingerplay, this time asking the children to join you.

4. Repeat the fingerplay several times, substituting a new body part such as eyes, nose, ears, hair, neck, or cheeks for the word "chin."

Variations/Ways to Extend:

- Ask the children to look at their hands and count the fingers on each one. Discuss the care of hands: Wash them often, clip the nails, and keep the nails clean.

- Using crayons, assist the children in tracing their hands on paper. Display these around the room.

- Help the students make handprints in plaster of Paris, clay, or flour dough. Here is an easy recipe for flour dough:

> 2 cups self-rising flour
> 2 tablespoons alum
> 2 tablespoons salt
> 2 tablespoons cooking oil
> 1 cup plus 2 tablespoons boiling water

Carefully mix all ingredients and then knead until a doughy consistency.

- Have the children make handprints using white poster paint on blue paper. You should make handprints, too, to compare them with the children's prints. (Be sure to have plenty of water and paper towels handy for cleaning up the work area and the children!)

I-10 HAPPY AND SAD FACES

Subject Area: Creative Dramatics/Movement

Concepts/Skills: Applies glue and pastes
Points to body parts (facial features)

Objective: The children will construct paper masks showing the emotions of joy and sadness.

Materials:
- Large white paper plates, one for each child with eye holes precut
- Happy and unhappy mouth shapes as well as a variety of nose shapes cut from construction paper
- Lengths of string
- 1″ pieces of yarn for hair
- Hole puncher
- Large mirror
- Glue or paste
- 4″ paper squares to hold glue

Procedure:

1. Discuss with the children things that make them happy or sad. Talk about how a person looks when he or she feels happy or sad.

2. Distribute one precut plate to each child. Let him or her paste a nose and either type of mouth on the mask.

3. Distribute the 1″ yarn strips. Have the children dip them into the glue on the four-inch paper squares and then place them on the top of the plate for hair.

4. Let the plates dry, punch holes on both sides of the plates, and attach the lengths of string.

5. Place the masks onto the children's faces and tie the strings around their heads. Allow the children to try on their masks and look at themselves in the mirror. Ask what the face shows—happiness or sadness. Describe a situation such as "You lost your mommy in the store" or "Daddy brought a surprise home for you" and ask the children which mask would show how they would feel.

Variations/Ways to Extend:

- Encourage the children to express a happy or sad face to match the mask you hold up. Have them look in the mirror to see if they look happy or sad.
- Another type of mask can be made by taping a tongue depressor to the bottom of each mask. The children can hold these up in front of their faces.

I–11   SHAPE BOY, SHAPE GIRL

Subject Area: Art

Concepts/Skills: Identifies own gender
Identifies boy and girl
Applies glue and pastes pieces

Objective: The children will assemble boy and girl figures from precut body shapes.

Materials:
- Colored construction paper
- Precut shapes for body parts for each child
- White glue and 4" paper squares to put glue on
- Fine-point markers

Procedure:

1. Prepare the body parts as shown in the illustrations.

2. Ask each child if he or she is a boy or girl. Name the boys in the class and the girls in the class.
3. Give each child an oval and help make a face on each one. Tell them they are making a girl or boy just like themselves.
4. Distribute hair made from colored paper to match their own hair color.
5. Provide the body parts starting with the trunk and working to the hands and feet to paste together one at a time. Discuss how many heads they have, eyes, ears, hands, legs, and so forth. Label each finished shape boy or girl with that child's name.
6. Make a wall display in which all of the paper boys and girls are holding hands.

Variations/Ways to Extend:

- Invite the children to stand next to one another according to the order shown on the wall display. Point out which shape dolls (boy or girl) are next to one another and assist the children in forming a circle accordingly. Play "Ring Around the Rosie" in this circle of friends.
- Read the award-winning book *Do You Want to Be My Friend?* by Eric Carle (New York: Harper & Row, Pub., 1971).

Weekly Subtheme: Friends and School

I-12 WHO'S IN SCHOOL TODAY?

Subject Area: Social Studies

Concepts/Skills: Refers to self by name
Is aware of printed name
Places shapes in, on, beside, and under

Objectives: The children will gain awareness of their written names and play a flannelboard game.

Materials:
- Schoolhouse shape cut from felt
- Felt shapes of different colors to represent each child, labeled with the child's name
- Flannelboard
- Tune to "Where Is Thumbkin?"

Procedure:

1. Place the schoolhouse shape on the flannelboard. Introduce the felt shapes on which children's names are printed. Hold up each shape. Then sing to the children,

   Where is Kyle? (*hold up shape*)
   Where is Kyle?

   Ask child to sing back,

   Here I am! (*child waves to teacher*)
   Here I am!

   Teacher sings,

   How are you this morning?

   Child sings back,

   Very well, I thank you.

   Teacher sings,

   Welcome to school!
   Welcome to school!

2. Give the felt shape to the child whose name was sung and direct him or her where to put it on the flannelboard. Use the prepositions "in," "on," "beside," and "under" to direct the child in placing the shape in relation to the schoolhouse.

Variation/Way to Extend:

- Cut a second set of shapes in the same colors as the first. Encourage each child to choose one from this set and match by color with the ones on the flannelboard.

Weekly Subtheme: Friends and School

I-13   BIG AND LITTLE

Subject Area: Math

Concepts/Skills: Points to big and little objects
Shows curiosity and interest in surroundings

Objectives: The children will talk about and sort some objects by size.

Materials: • Big and little shapes cut from oaktag
• Two decorated boxes, one small and one large

Procedure:

1. Draw or trace onto oaktag some simple shapes found around the school. Make two of each—one large and one small. Cut them out.
2. Discuss with the children the idea of big and little, and show them the shapes. Let each child take a turn selecting a shape and sorting it into the "big" box or the "little" box. Assist them and praise their efforts.

Variations/Ways to Extend:

• Do this activity with real objects if you have several pairs of items that are the same except for their size.
• Show the children a picture of a "big" teapot and a "little" teapot and teach them the following nursery song with the actions:

I'm a little teapot short and stout (*left hand on waist*).
Here is my handle, here is my spout (*right hand up in the air*).
When I get all steamed up, I just shout,
Tip me over and pour me out (*lean over to the right*).

I-14   WILL YOU BE A FRIEND OF MINE?

Subject Area: Music

Concepts/Skills: Finds own play area or activity
                          Repeats parts of a song

Objective: The children will learn a new song about friendship.

Material: • Words to the song (see Procedure section)

Procedure:

1. Explain to the children that we all have friends—friends at home and friends at school. Tell the students that this song will help them make new friends.

2. Have the students form a circle. Sing (to the tune of "London Bridge") the following song through a few times for the students, singing to particular children as you stand in the center of the circle:

    Will you be a friend of mine?
    Friend of mine? Friend of mine?
    Will you be a friend of mine
    And come along with me?

    Yes I'll be a friend of yours,
    Friend of yours, friend of yours,
    Yes I'll be a friend of yours
    And go along with you.

3. Approach pairs of children, clasp their hands together, and sing the song. Then send the two children to play together in another area of the room.

4. Be sure to send each pair of children to different activities around the room.

Variations/Ways to Extend:

• After the pairs of children have had time to play in their particular activities, call them back to the circle and play "Here We Go Looby Loo."

• Read a book about friends, such as *A Friend Is Someone Who Likes You* by Joan W. Anglund (San Diego: Harcourt Brace Jovanovich, Inc., 1958).

I–15   SCHOOL DAYS

Subject Area: Creative Dramatics/Movement

Concepts/Skills: Repeats parts of a song
Follows directions
Imitates actions
Associates use of common objects

Objectives: The children will observe and dramatize the actions to a new song.

Material: • Words to the song (see Procedure section)

Procedure:

1. Teach the children the following song (sung to the tune of "Here We Go 'Round the Mulberry Bush"):

   This is the way we walk to school,
   Walk to school, walk to school.
   This is the way we walk to school,
   Early in the morning.

   This is the way we hang up our coat . . . .
   This is the way we greet our friends . . . .
   This is the way we color with a crayon . . . .
   This is the way we bounce a ball . . . .
   (and so on)

   For the last four verses, the last line changes to:

   At nursery school in the morning.

2. Demonstrate the particular actions and have the children join in the pantomime.

Variations/Ways to Extend:

- Ask the children to suggest things they do at school and to act them out.
- Act out a school activity and have the children guess what you are doing.
- Have students act out activities done at home or out of doors.
- Read *The School* by John Burningham (New York: Harper & Row, Pub., 1975).

HARVEST TIME AND THE FARM

- ○ Colors
- ○ Foods
- ○ Farm and Farm Animals
- ○ Halloween

Weekly Subtheme: Colors

I–16 LEAF COSTUMES

Subject Area: Creative Dramatics/Movement

Concepts/Skills: Is aware of fall season
Associates the word "tree" with correct object
Expresses idea through body movement

Objectives: The children will wear costumes and dramatize leaves falling from trees.

Materials:
- Two sheets of 18″ by 24″ colored construction paper for each child
- Leaf patterns
- Markers
- Scissors
- Two 2″ by 10″ fall-colored paper strips (to match leaves) for each child

Procedure:

1. Take the children to watch a tree shed its leaves. Discuss the variety of colors seen.
2. Draw leaf patterns, trace them on large paper, and cut out two identical leaves for each child. Tape at the top with paper strips.
3. Show children how to put the costumes over their heads.
4. Talk about the colors of these paper leaves.
5. Discuss what the leaves do when the wind blows. Ask, "How do the leaves get on the ground?"
6. Explain how the trees change and the leaves turn color and fall to the ground.
7. Choose several children to put on the leaf costumes. Ask them the colors of the costumes they put on. Show them how to slowly crouch down as if they are leaves falling to the ground. Give all the children who are willing a turn falling like a leaf while wearing the costumes. Tell each color to fall at a different time.

Variations/Ways to Extend:

- Have the children sing "Ring Around the Rosie" with their costumes on, changing the one line to "the leaves fall down." At this point, call out a different color each time. Those children wearing that color fall down.
- Ask students to pretend they are leaves that lightly blow around the room and gently make a pile. Ask certain color leaves to do different things, reminding them of their color if they forget.
- Read *My Very First Book of Colors* by Eric Carle (New York: Harper & Row, Pub., 1974).

Weekly Subtheme: Colors

I-17 FALL WALK

Subject Area: Science

Concepts/Skills: Develops awareness of fall colors and seasonal changes
Follows a one-stage command
Begins to develop a sense of touch and smell
Begins to understand hard and soft, wet and dry

Objectives: The children will go on a nature walk and collect and sort found objects.

Materials: • Brown paper bags
• Display table

Procedure:

1. Read a book about fall, such as *Now It's Fall* by Lois Lenski (New York: Walck, 1948), or discuss the signs of fall: colors, sounds, smells, and textures.

2. Take the class on a walk and point out the things that tell us it is fall, such as colored leaves, nuts, milkweed pods, and so forth.

3. Encourage the children to collect a few leaves, acorns, moss, and so forth and place them in their bags to bring back to school. While walking, talk about the cooler temperatures, the birds flying south, the color of the leaves, and so on.

4. When they return to class have them take turns showing their favorite pieces in their collections. After they show them, place them on a display table. Ask questions as they show them: "What is the main color of your leaf?" "Which objects are hard?" "Which are soft?" "Which are wet?" "Dry?" "Which ones get used by animals (in the woods)?"

Variations/Ways to Extend:

• If a fall walk is impossible, try to get fall pictures from calendars or magazines.
• Read the four-line poem "The Leaves Fall Down" by Margaret W. Brown from her book *Nibble, Nibble* (New York: Young Scott Books, 1959).
• Splatter paint around the leaves on white paper. Use fall colors for the paint.

Weekly Subtheme: Colors

I–18 FALL SPONGE PAINTING

Subject Area: Art

Concepts/Skills: Develops fine motor skills
Identifies color
Expresses creativity

Objective: The children will create sponge prints of leaf shapes.

Materials:
- Sponges cut in triangles and rectangles
- Small dishes for paint
- Yellow, red, orange, and brown poster paints
- 11" by 18" sheets of manila paper
- Paintbrush

Procedure:

1. Encourage each child to make a tree trunk and branches on manila paper using brown paint. Let dry.
2. Demonstrate how to dip the sponges in the fall colored paints and then press on paper to make "the leaves" on the tree.
3. Discuss the paint colors in the dishes. To keep colors distinct, provide several sponges for each color so that the children will not use the same sponge for different colors.
4. Print leaves in all the different colors on the tree. Let it dry and then display in the room.

Variations/Ways to Extend:

- Cut a leaf shape from a sponge to use as a print.
- Cut a leaf shape from a potato half for printing. Or cut a leaf shape from rubber tubing and glue onto a thin piece of wood for a rubber stamp.
- Makes trees to show the four seasons: green leaves for summer, fall colored leaves for autumn, bare branches for winter, and buds and blossoms for spring.

I–19 LEAVES OF MANY COLORS

Subject Area: Language Arts

Concepts/Skills: Is aware of signs of fall
Imitates actions
Repeats parts of a fingerplay

Objectives: The children will recall the words and act out a fingerplay.

Materials: • Fall pictures showing colored leaves, apples, and so on
• Sheer, colored scarves

Procedure:

1. Remind the children of the fall walk they took. Ask them to think again of what they saw. Show the fall pictures to help remind them.

2. Teach the following fingerplay:

    Fall winds begin to blow (*purse lips to blow*).
    Colored leaves fall fast and slow (*flutter hands down*)
    Whirling, twirling all around (*turn yourself around*),
    And at last, they touch the ground (*touch the floor*).

3. Demonstrate the actions to each line and invite the children to imitate you. Repeat this several times.

4. Distribute sheer, colored scarves to the children and have them twirl them around during the fingerplay.

Variations/Ways to Extend:

• Make baked apples using the recipe given here. A toaster oven may be used if a regular oven is not available. (**Caution:** To be done only under adult supervision.)

    Preheat the oven to 375° F.
    Use several baking apples, such as Rome, Winesap, Starr, Jersey Red, or Greening.
    Core the apples and remove a 1″ strip of skin around the middle or pare the upper half of each apple.
    Place the apples upright in a baking dish and pour ½ cup of water around them.
    Fill the center of each apple with 1 tablespoon of honey, chopped raisins, 1 teaspoon of butter or margarine, and ⅛ teaspoon of cinnamon.
    Bake 30 to 40 minutes or until tender.
    Cool and enjoy sharing.

• Print the fingerplay on a sheet of paper or thermal master and make copies for the children to bring home and share with their families. Be sure to include simple illustrations showing the actions.

I-20 PUMPKIN MUFFINS

Subject Area: Nutrition/Foods Experience

Concepts/Skills: Identifies the color orange
Begins to develop a sense of smell

Objectives: The children will help to mix and bake pumpkin muffins.

Materials:
- Oven or toaster oven
- Muffin pans
- Grater
- Cooling rack
- Pot holders
- Large stainless steel mixing bowl
- Spatula and large spoon
- Pumpkin for display
- Measuring spoons
- Measuring cup
- Whole nutmegs and cinnamon bark
- Shortening to grease pans
- Small pot to melt butter or margarine
- Napkins or small plates
- Ingredients for pumpkin muffins

Procedure:

1. Show the pumpkin to the children and explain how it grows on a vine in a farmer's field.

2. Identify the color orange. Let the students think of other items or things that are orange. Talk about the pumpkin's shape and let the children feel it. Explain that the pumpkin can be cooked and eaten like other fruits.

3. Let the children smell the spices and then carefully try grating the whole nutmegs and cinnamon bark on a small grater.

4. Help the children to compare the cooked canned pumpkin with the actual pumpkin. Tell them they are going to make pumpkin muffins.

5. Follow this basic recipe for twelve muffins. Let as many children as possible help measure the ingredients and stir the batter.

> 1½ cups all-purpose flour
> ½ cup sugar or honey
> 2 teaspoons baking powder
> ½ teaspoon salt
> ½ teaspoon cinnamon
> 1 egg
> ½ cup milk
> ½ cup canned pumpkin
> ¼ cup butter or margarine, melted
> ½ teaspoon nutmg

Preheat the oven to 400° F. (**Caution:** To be done only under teacher's supervision.) Grease the muffin pans. Measure and mix the ingredients—batter should be lumpy. Fill the cups two-thirds full and sprinkle ¼ teaspoon of sugar over each muffin. Bake 18 to 20 minutes. Remove from pans, cool, and enjoy.

Variations/Ways to Extend:

- Recite the rhyme "The Muffin Man" while the muffins are cooling. Explain that the muffin man made and sold muffins like the bakery does today.

- Write a note to the children's parents and include the muffin recipe so that the families can try baking them at home.

- Eat the muffins outside while talking about the fall colors.

Weekly Subtheme: Foods

I-21 FALL FOODS BOOK

Subject Area: Art

Concepts/Skills: Applies glue
Matches two color samples

Objective: The children will construct a booklet showing various foods of the fall season.

Materials:
- Colored construction paper in fall colors
- Markers
- Glue
- Stapler
- A large variety of precut magazine pictures of foods (seed catalogs and gourmet magazines are good sources)
- A few fresh fruits or vegetables

Procedure:

1. Discuss foods bought at the market. Allow the children to smell, touch, and taste the foods.
2. Let each child choose a few of the food pictures. Talk about the foods shown and help each child choose sheets of paper that correspond to the colors of their foods, such as orange for a carrot picture and red for an apple picture.
3. Have the children paste their pictures onto the separate sheets of paper.
4. Staple these sheets into a booklet for each child.

Variations/Ways to Extend:

- In the art area, draw (on easel paper) fruit and vegetable shapes for the children to paint.
- Add scratch-and-sniff stickers to the food book, or use a drop of food flavoring on each page for them to sniff and identify. (Mint, lemon, orange, banana, and maple are some suggestions.)
- Make picture cards to represent fall foods and ask the children to identify them.
- Make a food bulletin board emphasizing the foods eaten in the fall.

I-22   PUSSY-CAT SALAD

Subject Area: Nutrition/Foods Experience

Concepts/Skills: Begins to develop a sense of touch, smell, and taste
Repeats parts of songs, rhymes, and fingerplays

Objectives: The children will listen to a nursery rhyme and then prepare and eat a salad snack.

Materials:
- Paper plates
- Forks
- Knife
- Paper bag
- Cottage cheese
- Carrots
- Raisins
- Apples
- Grapes

Procedure:

1. Tell the children the nursery rhyme, "Pussy-Cat, Where Have You Been?"

   Pussy-cat, pussy-cat, where have you been?
   I've been to London to visit the Queen.
   Pussy-cat, pussy-cat, what did you do there?
   I frightened a little mouse under the chair.

2. Explain to the children that they are going to make a pussy-cat salad with the items you have in a bag.

3. Keep the foodstuffs in their original containers and packages in the bag. Allow different children to take turns reaching in and removing one item at a time. Elicit descriptions of the foods as they remove each item from the bag. Talk about what it is, its color, where it comes from, and so forth.

4. Give each child a small mound of cottage cheese on a plate. Wash and prepare the other foods. Assist the children in adding raisin eyes, grape noses, carrot stick whiskers, and apple wedge ears to make kitten faces.

5. Eat them for snack time and talk about cats being found on farms and their popularity as home pets.

Variations/Ways to Extend:

- Make calico cats by giving each child a precut paper cat shape. The children use cut-up fabric scraps to paste all over, adding two button eyes, yarn whiskers, and a little bell strung on a piece of yarn and tied around the cat's neck.
- Show pictures of calico cats or bring in a stuffed calico cat toy.

I-23 FRUIT AND VEGGIE TOSS

Subject Area: Gross Motor Games

Concepts/Skills: Points to common object on command
Throws a small object two feet

Objective: The children will participate in a game using fall foods.

Materials:
- Plastic fruits and vegetables
- Masking tape
- Large fruit basket

Procedure:

1. Make a tape line on the floor about 1' in length.
2. Measure 2' away.
3. Each child takes a turn pointing to the plastic food piece you mention and picking it up. They then stand behind the tape line and try to throw it into the basket.

Variations/Ways to Extend:

- Hide the fruits and vegetables and have the children try to find them. Give hints using positional words such as "next to," "under," and so forth.
- Place a real fruit or vegetable in a bag or "feely box" and let a child guess what it is. Repeat with other food shapes.

I-24 THE APPLE TREE

Subject Area: Language Arts

Concepts/Skills: Points to common object
Imitates actions of adults
Repeats parts of a fingerplay

Objectives: The children will learn and recall the words to a new fingerplay about apples.

Materials:
- Picture or a color drawing of an apple tree
- Apples
- Words to the fingerplay (see Procedure section)

Procedure:

1. Show the picture of an apple tree. (Use the illustration shown here if needed.) Talk about apples, their color, shape, and taste. Discuss what can be made from them—applesauce, apple pie, candy apples, and so forth. Talk about how we get the apples down from the tree.

2. Introduce the following fingerplay in which the children can pretend they are shaking an apple off the tree:

   Way up in the apple tree (*reach up with both arms overhead*),
   Two little apples smiled at me (*touch fingers to thumbs in circle shapes*).
   I shook that tree as hard as I could (*hands around trunk—shake*)!
   Down came the apples (*arms and hands fall down*).
   Mmm they were good! (*lick lips and rub tummy*).

Variations/Ways to Extend:

- Visit an apple orchard or a neighboring yard that has apple or crab apple trees.
- Make a felt apple tree and have the children add red felt apples.
- Enjoy apple slices for a snack. Show the children the seeds inside when you slice the apple. Slice it horizontally to discover the "star" inside the apple.

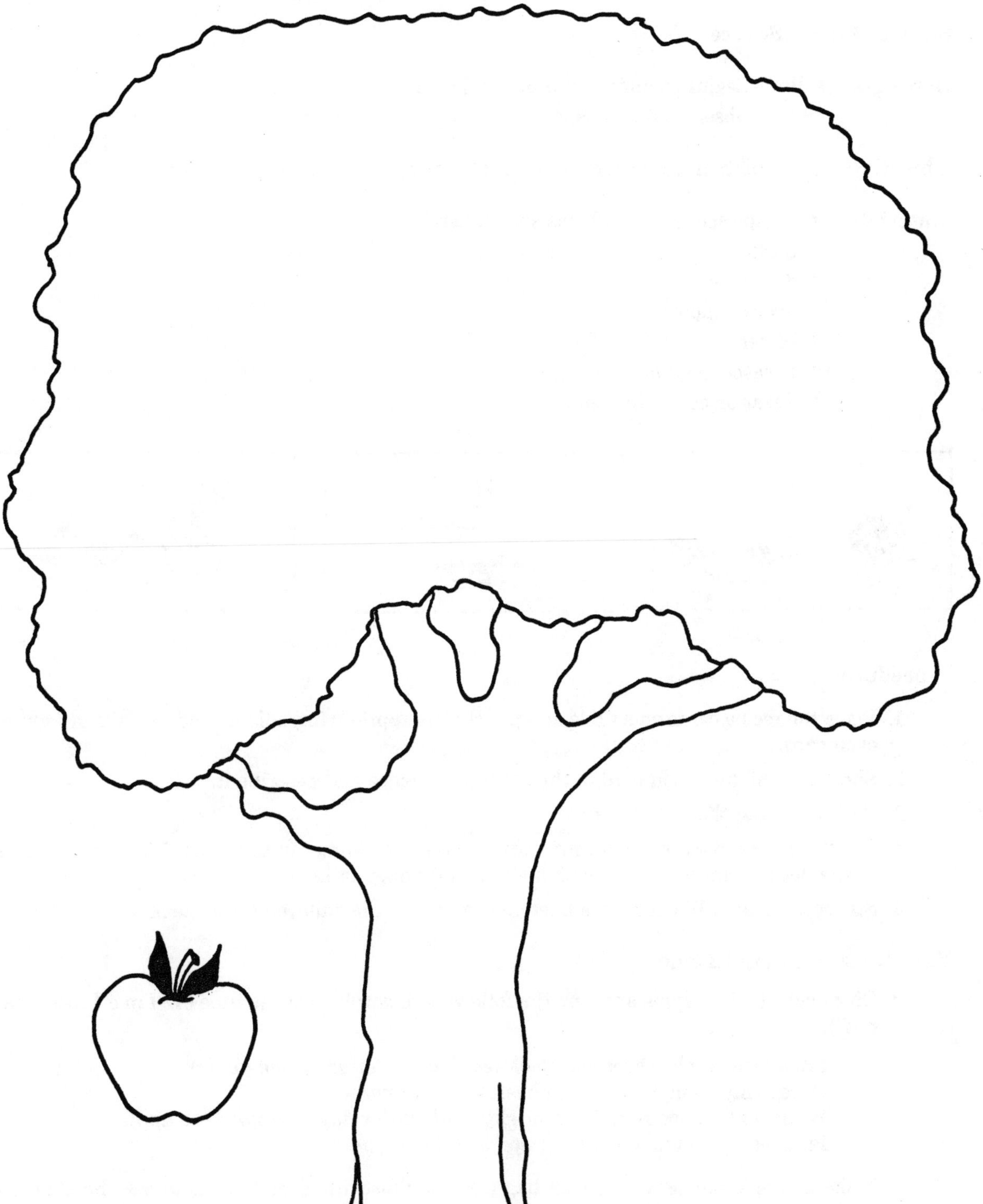

Weekly Subtheme: Foods

I-25 MAKING APPLESAUCE

Subject Area: Science

Concepts/Skills: Begins to understand hot and cold
Observes food change from one state to another

Objective: The children will participate in cooking apples to make applesauce.

Materials:
- Recipe sequence cards (as shown here)
- Fork
- Saucepan
- Six red apples
- Water
- 1 teaspoon cinnamon
- Sugar or honey to taste

Procedure:

1. Place the recipe cards on a table and put the appropriate ingredients and utensils in front of each card.
2. Show the children each card in the correct sequence and describe it.
3. Peel, core, and slice the apples.
4. Put the apples in a saucepan with a little water and simmer until tender. Mash the mixture to the desired consistency. Add cinnamon and honey to taste.
5. Stir occasionally. When finished, let cool. Serve to the children for a snack.

Variations/Ways to Extend:

- Give each child an apple and sing the following fingerplay (to the tune of "I'm a Little Teapot"):

  I'm a little apple, short and sleek (*each child holds up the apple*).
  Here is my stem, here is my cheek (*point to parts*).
  When you see me round and bright (*slide index finger around the apple*),
  Pick me up and take a bite (*pretend to take a bite*).

- Make an apple puppet on a lunch bag (see the illustration) and use it to ask the children questions about making applesauce.

Weekly Subtheme: Farm and Farm Animals

I-26   LET'S PLAY FARM

Subject Area: Social Studies

Concepts/Skills: Matches objects
Knows the names of three animals

Objectives: The children will observe pictures of farm animals and engage in dramatic play with a farm set.

Materials:
- Class trip arrangements
- Play farm set
- Farm pictures showing barn, animals, and farmer or a farm story
- Book (see Procedure section)

Procedure:

1. Show the pictures in the *Big Red Barn* by Margaret Wise Brown (Reading, Mass.: Addison-Wesley, 1956). Show the barn and describe how it is used. Let the children try to identify the plastic animals and have the group repeat the animal names. Explain that the job of a farmer is to care for the animals and provide food and shelter for them.

2. Provide another set of plastic animals. Allow the children to find two of the same and match them.

3. If possible, visit a farm or the farm section of a zoo. Let the children name the different animals and listen for the sounds they make. Point out the colors and sizes of the animals.

Variations/Ways to Extend:

- Use farm animal stickers on the children's papers this week.
- Enjoy milk and animal-shaped cookies for snacks. Help the children to identify the various animals.
- Let the children pretend they are different farm animals by walking on their hands and feet and making animal noises.
- Tape animal sounds and let the children identify which animal makes each sound.
- Read *Early Morning in the Barn* by Nancy Tafuri (New York: Greenwillow, 1983).

Weekly Subtheme: Farm and Farm Animals

I–27 THE COW IS BIG

Subject Area: Language Arts

Concepts/Skills: Points to big and little cows
Repeats parts of a fingerplay

Objectives: The children will observe a picture of a cow and repeat a fingerplay about cows.

Materials: • Words and actions to fingerplay (see Procedure section)
• Pictures of a cow and a calf

Procedure:

1. Show the pictures of the cow and calf. Point out that the cow is big, the calf is little. Ask the children to do the same. Remind the children that we get milk from a cow.

2. Teach the following fingerplay:

    The cow is big (*arms go out at sides*).
    Her eyes are round (*cup hands around eyes*).
    She makes a very scary sound (*look frightened*).
    I'm very glad that the fence is tall (*arms overhead*)
    Because I am so young and small (*bend knees*).

3. Ask the children to join you as you repeat the fingerplay several times.

Variations/Ways to Extend:

• Encourage the children to walk on all fours and moo like cows.
• Make a tasting table of foods that come from cows: milk, buttermilk, cheese, whipped cream, ice cream, butter, and beef.
• Secure a piece of cowhide and let the children touch and feel it. Show something, such as a belt or pocketbook, made from tanned cowhide.
• Read the poem "Cow" by Varlie Worth, found in her book *Small Poems* (New York: Farrar, Straus & Giroux, 1972).

Weekly Subtheme: Farm and Farm Animals

I-28 BAA, BAA BLACK SHEEP

Subject Area: Language Arts

Concepts/Skills: Understands the concept of "one"
Begins to understand sense of touch
Repeats parts of a rhyme

Objectives: The children will learn a nursery rhyme and make observations about sheep and wool.

Materials:
- Flannelboard
- Picture or drawing of black sheep backed with flannel
- Wool yarn or wool sweater
- Three bags of wool pictures or drawings backed with flannel and labeled as shown here.

Procedure:

1. Introduce the figure of a black sheep on the flannelboard. Remind the children that sheep live on a farm.
2. Make the "baa" sound of a sheep. Let them all repeat the sound.
3. Tell them that the sheep shares his coat with us. He has a woolly coat and farmers cut or shear it off.
4. Show a wool sweater; explain that the sweater is made from the wool yarn.
5. Show the flannelboard figures and explain that the farmer cuts the sheep's coat and puts the wool in bags.
6. Say the following nursery rhyme as you point to the figures. Call attention to the rhyming words. Have the children repeat it several times.

Baa, baa, black sheep	One for my master,
Have you any wool?	One for my dame,
Yes sir, yes sir,	One for the little boy,
Three bags full.	Who lives down the lane.
	(Repeat first stanza.)

Variations/Ways to Extend:

- Invite a farmer or county zookeeper to bring in a lamb for the children to see and feel.
- Let the children walk on all fours and "baa" like sheep.
- Make lamb pictures and glue cotton or lamb's wool on each coat.
- Listen to the record album *Mother Goose Suite* (available from Children's Music Center, 5373 W. Pico Boulevard, Los Angeles, Calif. 90019).

Weekly Subtheme: Farm and Farm Animals

I-29 SHEEP PUPPET

Subject Area: Art

Concepts/Skills: Applies glue and pastes pieces
Counts to two
Describes what happened in two or three words

Objective: The children will construct sheep puppets from paper bags.

Materials:
- One brown lunch bag for each child
- Sample sheep head (see the pattern shown here)
- Black construction paper for heads (one for each child)
- Two blue (and other colors) paper circles for eyes (two for each child)
- One pink paper nose for each child
- Lamb's wool or cotton
- Glue
- Marker

Procedure:

1. Give each child a lunch bag, flap frontward. Have one child's name already printed on each bag.

2. Give the children a black paper head and help them glue it to the bottom of the bag that makes the flap.

3. Distribute two eyes to each child. Let the children count them and tell you the color. Then have the children paste the eyes in place.

4. Distribute a small amount of lamb's wool or cotton to each child, and let them feel it and describe it. Ask the students to paste it on the top of the sheep's head. Let the glue dry.

5. Next have the children put the puppets on their hands and say, "I made a sheep." (See the illustration for a sample puppet.)

6. Recite the nursery rhyme "Baa, Baa, Black Sheep" while the children wear their puppets.

Variations/Ways to Extend:

- Make bag puppets of several other farm animals. Let the children pretend they are the animals and make the animal sounds.
- Let the children make a fabric collage using different yarn scraps and lamb's wool.
- Let the children make a simple sheep puzzle cut from a picture or work with farm animal wooden puzzles available commercially.

I–30 HELLO TO THE ANIMALS

Subject Area: Music

Concepts/Skills: Appreciates and participates in music
Distinguishes between loud and soft
Places large puzzle pieces in appropriate slots

Objectives: The children will sing a song and recall the sounds that various farm animals make.

Materials:
- Words and music to "Hello to the Animals" (see next page)
- Farm pictures showing a farmer and animals
- "Farm Animals" puzzle

Procedure:

1. Show the pictures of the farm animals, including cows, pigs, horses, and hens.
2. Talk about the animal names and the sounds they make.
3. Sing "Hello to the Animals" once. Then sing it again and ask the children to join in on the animal sounds.
4. Now sing the song together. Sing some of the animal sounds loudly and other sounds softly, pointing out the difference to the children.
5. Continue the song using other animals and sounds if the children suggest some.

Variations/Ways to Extend:

- Make a tape recording of the children singing the song and play it back for them.
- Order the five-piece puzzle "Farm Animals" from Judy Instructional Aids, The Judy Company, 250 James Street, Morristown, N.J. 07960.
- Sing "Old MacDonald Had a Farm" and have the children sing some animal sounds loudly and others softly.
- Read a story about farm animals. One suggestion is *Good Morning, Chick* by Mirra Ginsburg (New York: Greenwillow, 1980).

Hello to the Animals

Words and Music by BOB MESSANO
Arranged by John Sheehan

Vivace (♩ = 160)

1. I went to the barn to milk the cow but my ma - ma nev - er told me how— The cow said, "Moo, moo!" I said, "Hel - lo!"

Copyright 1984 Bob Messano

2. I went to the barn to feed the pig,
   He got up and did a jig!
   The pig said, 'Oink, Oink!"
   (And) I said, "Hello!"

3. I went to the barn to see my horse,
   She ran off to the old racecourse.
   The horse said, "Nay, Nay!"
   (And) I said "Hello!"

4. I went to the barn to see my hen;
   She hasn't laid an egg since I don't know when!
   The hen said, "Cluck, Cluck!"
   (And) I said, "Hello!"

I–31 JACK-O'-LANTERN

Subject Area: Social Studies

Concepts/Skills: Shows pleasure in dealing with people and things
Begins to understand wet and dry

Objective: The children will learn about the custom of a jack-o'-lantern.

Materials:
- Medium to large pumpkin
- Permanent marker
- Sharp knife
- Newspapers
- Bowl
- Large spoon
- Small flashlight

Procedure:

1. Show the children the pumpkin. Discuss its color and shape, and explain where and how pumpkins grow.

2. Place newspaper on the work table and set a bowl for pumpkin seeds nearby.

3. Cut off the top of the pumpkin and scoop out the pulp and seeds. (**Caution:** Handle the knife carefully in front of the children.) Allow the children to notice the wet, stringy substance. Save the seeds in a bowl.

4. Ask the children what kind of face they want you to draw on the pumpkin. Should it be happy? Sad? Silly? Mad? Draw on one of these types with the marker. Then cut out the eyes, nose, and mouth.

5. Tell the children the pumpkin is now called a jack-o'-lantern, which means a "Jack of light."

6. Turn on a flashlight and place it at the bottom of the hollowed-out pumpkin. Darken the room and let the pumpkin glow.

Variations/Ways to Extend:

- Read *Mousekin's Golden House* by Edna Miller (Englewood Cliffs, N.J.: Prentice-Hall, 1964).

- Have the children sing while they watch the jack-o'-lantern glow. Sing the following words to the tune of "This Is the Way":

    I saw a pumpkin face so glad (mad, sad, scared),
       face so glad, face so glad.
    I saw a pumpkin face so glad.
    It's Halloween in October.

- Spread the leftover pumpkin seeds in a single layer on a cookie sheet and let them **dry** thoroughly. When dry, let the children glue the seeds onto construction paper to form a design or picture. Display this for the students to see.

Weekly Subtheme: Halloween

I–32   JACK-O'-LANTERN FRUIT SALAD

Subject Area: Nutrition/Foods Experience

Concepts/Skills: Begins to develop a sense of touch, smell, and taste
Follows simple directions

Objectives: The children will help to prepare a fruit salad and enjoy eating it from a special container.

Materials:
- One thick-skinned orange for each child
- Bananas
- Seedless grapes
- Apples
- Sharp knife
- Paring knife
- Blunt knives
- Paper plates
- Spoons

Procedure:

1. Slice off the tops of the oranges. Scoop out the orange fruit and set aside.
2. Carefully cut out jack-o'-lantern expressions on the oranges using the sharp knife.
3. Let the children peel and slice the bananas with a blunt knife. (**Caution:** Be sure the children are supervised during this step.) Let the children wash and drain the grapes.
4. Core and slice the apples yourself.
5. Let the children mix the fruit sections with the reserved orange fruit and fill each individual orange jack-o'-lantern.

Variations/Ways to Extend:

- Make a picture lotto game of the fruits used in the salad. Divide a large sheet of paper into quarters and draw a picture of an apple in one, a banana in another, grapes in another, and an orange in the fourth. (Magazine pictures of the fruits could also be used.) Make picture cards to match and let the children take turns matching each picture to its correct place on the paper.
- Listen to "Mr. Jack-o'-Lantern" and "Trick or Treat" on *Happy Halloween* by Playskool (Polygram Records, Inc., 810 Seventh Avenue, New York, N.Y. 10019).

I-33 JACK-O'-LANTERN MASKS

Subject Area: Creative Dramatics/Movement

Concepts/Skills: Develops fine motor movements by pasting and painting
Learns parts of a face

Objectives: The children will finger-paint a mask and dramatize a Halloween rhyme.

Materials:
- One white paper plate for each child
- Glue
- Orange finger paint
- Water
- Eyes, noses, and smiling mouths made of black construction paper
- Stencil knife
- Cutting board
- Hole puncher
- String
- Large mirror

Procedure:

1. Wet the paper plates with a little water.
2. Place a dab of orange finger paint on each plate and let the children finger-paint.
3. Label each plate with the child's name and set the plates aside to dry.
4. When dry, return the plates to the children along with two eyes for each plate. Ask the children to glue these in place.
5. Now distribute a variety of noses and mouths, discussing each part. Help the children glue these in place.
6. Punch a hole on each side of the plate and thread the string through.
7. Place the mask on the cutting board and partially cut open the eyes, nose, and mouth with the stencil knife.
8. Place the child's mask on his or her face and tie the string.
9. While wearing their masks, guide the children in reciting the following rhyme:

   See my jack-o'-lantern
   Smiling out at you.
   You don't need to be afraid
   When I holler . . . BOO!

10. Provide a large mirror for the children to see their masked faces.

Variations/Ways to Extend:

- Let the children sit on the floor with their masks on as if they were in a pumpkin patch. Ask them to slowly stand up as if they were growing bigger. When they are standing as tall as they can, the children are ready for Halloween and should say "Boo!"
- Make cheese pumpkins for a snack. Cut slices of cheese into the shape of a pumpkin, using either a round cookie cutter or a pumpkin cookie cutter. Add raisins for the eyes, nose, and mouth.

I-34   HALLOWEEN NIGHT

Subject Area: Language Arts

Concepts/Skills: Understands the concept "round"
Repeats parts of a rhyme

Objective: The children will repeat a fingerplay about Halloween.

Materials: • Jack-o'-lantern or pumpkin
• Words and motions to fingerplay (see Procedure section)
• Large orange felt pumpkin with smile
• Flannelboard

Procedure:

1. Show the jack-o'-lantern or pumpkin. Discuss its round shape. Ask the children to make their arms go around.

2. Show students the large felt pumpkin and place it on the flannelboard. Ask them if the pumpkin's smile makes him look happy or sad.

3. Teach the following fingerplay:

   Here is a pumpkin, big and round (*hands form circle*).
   Here is a kitty cat, soft and brown (*fists on top of each other, two fingers up*).
   Here is an owl with big, wide eyes (*cup fingers around eyes*).
   Here is a witch, watch how she flies (*wave hands in flying motion through air*).

Variations/Ways to Extend:

• Let the children point out other objects in the room that are round.
• Read *My Very First Book of Shapes* by Eric Carle (New York: Harper & Row, Pub., 1974).

Weekly Subtheme: Halloween

I-35 PUMPKIN BAGS

Subject Area: Art

Concept/Skill: Paints with a large paintbrush

Objectives: The children will construct and paint paper bag pumpkins.

Materials:
- One brown lunch bag for each child
- Newspapers
- Rubber bands
- Orange, green, and black paints
- Paintbrushes

Procedure:

1. Ask each child to stuff the brown bag half full with newspaper.
2. Help them to twist the top to make a stem and secure with a rubber band.
3. Have the children paint the stem green and the pumpkin bag bottom orange. Let dry.
4. Now help the children paint black eyes, a nose, and a mouth. Let the pumpkins dry completely before the children use them.

Variations/Ways to Extend:

- Make a pumpkin patch display with the pumpkin bags and thick green yarn arranged like a vine with pumpkins. Explain how pumpkins grow.
- Hide one of the pumpkin bags and let the children find it.

HOME
AND FAMILY

○ My Family

○ My Home and Neighborhood

○ American Indians

○ Thanksgiving

Weekly Subtheme: My Family

I–36 A PICTURE OF ME

Subject Area: Social Studies

Concept/Skill: Correctly identifies a picture of self from a photo.

Objective: The children will be highlighted as important members of their families by having photographs of themselves taken and displayed.

Materials:
- Instant camera and film
- Baby photos of each child
- Scissors
- Posterboard
- Marker

Procedure:

1. Show photos of yourself as a baby, child, teenager, and adult. Ask the children if they can see the resemblance as you grew.

2. Several days prior to this lesson, send a note home to parents asking for a baby photo of their child. Be sure that parents do not send valuable, one-of-a-kind photos! Show the children's baby photos one by one and ask them to guess who is who.

3. Take an instant photo of each child and mount on posterboard. You might want to display the current photos on the bulletin board with an autumn leaves' design.

4. Underneath each child's current photo, place the matching baby photo. Use a marker to label the photos with the children's names.

Variation/Way to Extend:

- Read *Families Live Together* by Esther Meeks and Elizabeth Bagwell (Chicago: Follett, 1969).

I-37 WHO IS IN MY FAMILY?

Subject Area: Language Arts

Concepts/Skills: Identifies boy and girl
Names family members from pictures
Identifies own gender

Objective: The children will identify their family members.

Materials: • Felt silhouettes in black to represent family members (see next page for patterns)
• Flannelboard

Procedure:

1. Introduce the felt figures of family members and describe who they are. You might want to tell about your family and demonstrate with the figures.

2. Ask each child who is in his or her family and select the appropriate figures to place on the flannelboard. Talk about who is big, who is small, who are girls, who are boys, how many in the family, and so forth. Point out similarities and differences in families.

3. Ask the children to tell whether they are boys or girls.

Variations/Ways to Extend:

• Have the children bring in photographs of their families. Use them with large felt silhouettes for a bulletin display.

• Read *Little Fur Family* by Margaret Wise Brown (New York: Harper & Row, Pub., 1984).

Weekly Subtheme: My Family

I–38   FAMILY PICTURE TREE

Subject Area: Math

Concepts/Skills: Applies glue and pastes
Learns one-to-one correspondence

Objectives: The children will discuss families and construct a family picture tree.

Materials:
- Paper
- Pictures of family members cut from magazines
- Paste
- One tree shape for each child (see the pattern)
- Precut leaf shapes

Procedure:

1. Discuss the idea of a family—a group of people who live together and love and care for one another. Talk about who are the members of their families.

2. Give each child a tree and leaves and have them paste individual pictures of Daddies, Mommies, Brothers, and Sisters or a composition that reflects their particular family situation.

3. Encourage the children to count the pictures on the tree and relate the total to the number of members in their own families.

Variations/Ways to Extend:

- Make finger puppets by mounting the pictures on 2″ by 2″ squares of paper rolled and taped to fit the child's finger.
- Make another type of finger puppet by cutting out the individual sections of an egg carton and pasting the picture to the solid side, as shown here. The child's finger goes underneath.

- Read *Mother's Helper* by Helen Oxenbury (New York: Dial Press, 1982).

Weekly Subtheme: My Family

I-39 ROCK-A-BABY

Subject Area: Music

Concepts/Skills: Repeats parts of a song
Imitates actions of adults

Objective: The children will participate in an action song about families.

Materials:
- Words to "Rock-a-Bye-Baby"
- Dolls with blankets
- Pictures of families doing different things

Procedure:

1. Show the pictures and talk about the many things family members do alone and together.

2. Teach the following song to the children:

> Rock-a-bye-baby on the tree top.
> When the wind blows, the cradle will rock.
> When the bough breaks
> The cradle will fall,
> And down will come baby
> Cradle and all.

3. Each child can hold a doll wrapped in a blanket. While singing, the children can slowly cradle and rock their "babies."

Variations/Ways to Extend:

- Use dress-up clothes and props to dramatize the song.
- Read *Peggy's New Brother* by Eleanor Schick (New York: Macmillan, 1970).

Weekly Subtheme: My Family

I–40   CLOTHESPIN FAMILY

Subject Area: Art

Concepts/Skills: Becomes aware of clothing differences
Develops fine motor ability

Objective: The children will construct clothespin dolls.

Materials:
- Scissors
- Glue
- Cellophane tape
- Round-type clothespins
- Fabric scraps cut in squares and long rectangles
- Pipe cleaners
- Gauze squares
- Markers

Procedure:

1. Discuss clothing typically worn by different family members.
2. Let each child pick a fabric scrap and put a small slit in the middle of it for the clothespin head to fit through.
3. Use the squares to make shirts for the men and boys and rectangles to make long dresses for the women and girls. Put the white gauze squares between the slit at the base of the clothespin and tape around the middle to form a diaper for a baby.
4. Wrap a pipe cleaner around the neck to form the arms and around the waist as a belt if necessary. On male dolls, color base and legs with markers for pants.
5. Help each child make a face with the marker on each clothespin head.

Variations/Ways to Extend:

- Use the dolls to practice prepositions: Put the doll in, on, under, on top of the table, and so forth.
- Read *The Runaway Bunny* by Margaret Wise Broom (New York: Harper & Row, Pub., 1972).
- Listen to "Grandma's Glasses" and many other delightful fingerplays on *Fingerplay Fun* by Rosemary Hallum (Educational Activities, Inc., Box 392, Freeport, N.Y. 11520). The album contains the words, music, and directions for both newly popular and old favorite fingerplays.

Weekly Subtheme: My Home and Neighborhood

I–41 A NEIGHBORHOOD WALK

Subject Area: Social Studies

Concepts/Skills: Describes what happened in two or three words
Paints with a large brush
Begins to develop sense of touch, smell, hearing, and sight

Objectives: The children will use their senses to enjoy a neighborhood walk and later paint a picture reflecting the experience.

Materials:
• Camera for slides or snapshots
• Film

Procedure:

1. Introduce the word *neighborhood* and discuss children's neighborhood.
2. Discuss the walk you will take around the school neighborhood and stress following directions and safety rules along with the idea that they are to use all their senses to discover things on their walk.
3. Ask questions as you walk. Ask them how the grass smells or the color of the brook. How do the trees feel? What do they hear? Take pictures of things that interest them as you go.
4. When you return to class, ask them to recall what they saw, heard, touched, and smelled.
5. Use the experience as a stimulus for a painting at the easel. Ask the children to paint something they saw or paint the way something made them feel.

Variations/Ways to Extend:

• When the pictures are developed, use them to discuss and review the walk.
• Make a miniphoto album of the pictures.

I–42 TWO LITTLE HOUSES

Subject Area: Language Arts

Concepts/Skills: Repeats parts of a fingerplay
Shows pleasure in dealing with people and things

Objective: The children will participate in a fingerplay about houses and people.

Material: • Words to fingerplay (see Procedure section)

Procedure:

1. Introduce the following fingerplay to the children:

    Two little houses closed up tight (*fists closed, thumbs closed in*).
    Open up the window and let in the light (*fingers and thumbs stretched*).
    Ten little finger people, tall and straight (*palms to the front, fingers erect*)
    Ready for nursery school, and don't be late!

2. Repeat the fingerplay several times with the children.

Variation/Way to Extend:

• Help the children use unit blocks to build houses in a neighborhood. Use props such as masking-tape streets, toy cars, plastic or paper trees, and dollhouse people if desired.

I–43 HOUSEHOLD SOUNDS

Subject Area: Science

Concepts/Skills: Begins to develop a sense of hearing
Identifies loud and soft sounds

Objective: The children will observe the sounds made by various household items.

Materials: • Household objects—wooden spoons, metal spoons, pans and lids, egg beaters, sandpaper, bells, timers, and so forth
• Large basket

Procedure:

1. Provide a basket full of household objects each of which makes a distinctive sound.
2. Allow the children access to these for exploration of sound. Point out contrasts of loud and soft.
3. Note the differences made by the same object when held in the hand, placed on the table while heads are up, and on the table while ears are pressed to the table. Which is loudest?

Variations/Ways to Extend:

• Listen to the Hap Palmer album entitled *Homemade Band,* available from Educational Activities, Inc., Freeport, N.Y. 11520. Pay particular attention to the songs "Can You Make a Sound?" and "Make a Pretty Sound."
• Set up a cardboard box on a table. Stand behind the box and use different objects to produce various sounds. Ask the children to try to guess what object is making each particular sound.
• Read *Pigs Say Oink: First Book of Sounds* by Martha Alexander (New York: Random House, 1981).
• Listen to the album *The Counting Color and Sound ABC's* (Wonderland Records, Division of A. A. Records, Inc., Dept. WR, 1105 Globe Avenue, Mountainside, N.J. 07092).

I-44   FLY, LITTLE BLUEBIRD

Subject Area: Music

Concepts/Skills: Repeats parts of a song
Jumps or hops
Follows directions

Objectives: The children will participate in a song and game about windows and gardens.

Material: • Words to song (see Procedure section)

Procedure:

1. Sing the following song to the tune of "Skip to My Lou":

    Fly, little bluebird, through my window.
    Fly, little bluebird, through my window.
    Fly, little bluebird, through my window.
    Um diddle um dum dey.

    Hop, little bluebird, in my garden.
    Hop, little bluebird, in my garden.
    Hop, little bluebird, in my garden.
    Um diddle um dum dey.

2. Have the children form a circle while holding hands with arms raised to make windows while singing the first verse.

3. Select one child to be the bluebird who goes in and out of the windows and then hops or jumps inside the circle ("the garden").

4. You or the child select the next bluebird to begin the song again until each child has had a turn as bluebird.

Variation/Way to Extend:

• Read *A Little House of Your Own* by Beatrice S. DeRegniers and Irene Haas (San Diego: Harcourt Brace Jovanovich, Inc., 1955).

Weekly Subtheme: My Home and Neighborhood

I–45 HOUSE COLLAGE

Subject Area: Art

Concepts/Skills: Names common pictured objects
Applies glue and pastes collage pieces

Objectives: The children will talk about household items and construct a collage.

Materials:
- Construction paper for each child cut in the shape of a house
- Magazine pictures of household objects
- Paste
- Fabric scraps

Procedure:

1. Provide an assortment of magazine pictures of household objects. Hold these up and ask the children to identify them and point out certain objects that you name.

2. Have the children select objects they want and paste these onto the paper house.

3. Using fabric scraps, have the children also paste around the picture collage items that they would like to have in their house.

Variations/Ways to Extend:

- Read *I Spy With My Little Eye: A Picture Book of Objects in a Child's Home Environment* by Lucille Ogle (New York: McGraw-Hill, 1970).

- Cut and fold construction paper, as shown here, to make a house with a front door. Ask the children to paste on an appropriate number of silhouettes to represent the number of family members in their homes. The children can decorate the house with fabric scraps if desired.

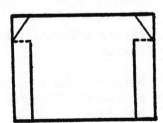

I–46 FEATHER DECORATIONS

Subject Area: Social Studies

Concepts/Skills: Colors with crayons
Shows curiosity and interest in surroundings

Objective: The children will decorate small baskets in a way similar to that of American Indians.

Materials:
- Crayons
- 4″ paper feathers
- Small plastic produce baskets, the kind in which strawberries or cherry tomatoes are sold
- American Indian posters and pictures

Procedure:

1. Introduce the children to American Indians by showing pictures and posters obtained from the organizations listed below.

2. Explain to the children that American Indians of the West Coast created beautiful baskets from woven reeds and grasses and decorated them with shells and feathers. They used these baskets to gather acorns (to make flour), wild berries, seeds, and nuts.

3. Give each child several paper feathers to decorate with crayons.

4. When the feathers are completed, give each child a small plastic basket. Help the children to weave (or tape) the feathers around the sides of the basket.

5. Use these baskets on a nature walk to collect acorns, twigs, and small rocks.

Variation/Way to Extend:

- Help the children create clay pinch pots. Allow the pinch pots to dry thoroughly before painting them.

Special Note: Use the terms *American Indians* or *Native Americans* when teaching this and the following lessons. Be sensitive to stereotyping of American Indians by avoiding such phrases as "Sit like an Indian" or "Hop like an Indian."

The activities found in this section attempt to introduce some of the richness of the American Indian culture. Realize, however, that there are over 200 nations, each one separate and distinct.

More information on teaching about Native Americans can be obtained by writing to:

Council on Interracial Books for Children
1841 Broadway
New York, N.Y. 10023
(Ask for *Unlearning "Indian" Stereotypes* and *Books for Equity*.)

Mohawk Nation
Rooseveltown, N.Y. 13683
(Ask for posters, booklists, and "Akwesasne Notes.")

Instructor Publications
Danville, N.Y. 14437
(Ask for prints, teacher guides, posters, and a catalog.)

Native American Educational Program
P.S. 199
West 107 Street
New York, N.Y. 10025
(Ask for information about posters and records.)

Museum of the American Indian
Broadway at 155 Street
New York, N.Y. 10032
(Ask for information on slides, books, and a catalog.)

I–47 STONES AND FEATHERS

Subject Areas: Language Arts and Science

Concept/Skill: Begins to understand hard and soft

Objectives: The children will participate in a game and identify hard and soft materials.

Materials:
- Stones
- Wool
- Cotton
- Feathers
- Clay
- Tree bark

Procedure:

1. Explain to the children that Northwest American Indians used sharp *stones* to cut pictures into wood. They used *wool* and *cotton* to make blankets and shirts. The Plains Indians used *feathers* for decorating baskets and bonnets. Pueblo Indians created jars and bricks from *clay*. Woodland Indians used *tree bark* (and logs) to make homes.

2. Display the following hard materials: stones, dried clay, and tree bark; and these soft materials: wool, cotton, and feathers.

3. Play a guessing game with the children. First show each material, identify it, and tell if it is hard or soft. Then allow the children to feel each one. Ask each child to take turns in closing his or her eyes, feeling one of the materials, and stating if it is hard or soft.

Variation/Way to Extend:

- Collect classroom objects and continue the game described above, allowing the children to identify hard and soft.

I-48 LET'S WEAR NECKLACES

Subject Area: Art

Concepts/Skills: Explores new materials
Develops fine motor movement of stringing clay beads

Objective: The children will construct a necklace made of clay beads.

Materials:
- Clay (made from recipe)
- Plastic straws
- Tongue depressors
- Cellophane tape
- Bottle caps
- Tempera paint
- Yarn
- Scissors

Procedure:

1. Explain to the children that the Navajo Indians traded buffalo hides for blue turquoise stones to create attractive necklaces. Let the children know that they can make similar representations of these necklaces with clay beads.

2. Provide each child with a mound of clay made out of this recipe:

   1 cup cornstarch
   1½ cups water
   2 cups baking soda
   pinch of salt

   Mix the ingredients in a saucepan and stir over medium heat until thick. Place on wax paper and let cool, kneading until smooth. Place in a moist towel and refrigerate for approximately 15 minutes. (*Note*: Clay that is not used for beads will remain soft if kept in a closed plastic bag with a small amount of water and in a refrigerator.)

3. Allow the children to experiment with the clay. Provide plastic straws, tongue depressors, bottle caps, and other items. Encourage rolling, poking, and pinching.

4. Assist the children in making necklace beads by rolling the clay into several small balls and pushing a plastic straw through each one to make a hole.

5. Allow the beads to dry overnight. The following day, let the children paint the beads with blue (for turquoise look) or any other colors they want.

6. Cut the yarn into 30″ lengths, wrap one end with tape for a stringing needle, and tie a knot in the other end.

7. After the beads are dry, assist the children in creating a necklace by stringing the yarn through the beads.

Variations/Ways to Extend:

- Make colorful macaroni necklaces by adding one teaspoon of vinegar and a few drops of food coloring to each bowl of water representing the primary colors. Place a cup of elbow macaroni or ziti macaroni in each bowl. Soak for 5 to 10 minutes, then drain on paper towels. When the macaroni is dry, give each child several of each color to string on the yarn for a necklace following the procedure above.

- For variety, you might have the children string both colored macaroni and clay beads to form designs and patterns for necklaces and bracelets.

I–49   CORNBREAD

Subject Area: Nutrition/Foods Experience

Concepts/Skills: Develops fine motor skills of measuring, pouring, and mixing
Shows curiosity and interest in surroundings

Objectives: The children will participate in preparing and baking cornbread.

Materials:
- Indian corn for display
- Cornbread mix, water, and eggs (or cornbread recipe*)
- Measuring cups and spoons
- Pan
- Toaster oven or oven

Procedure:

1. Discuss the Indian corn and how the Indians taught the Pilgrims to grow corn, make popcorn, and flour for cornbread.
2. Let the children help to measure, pour, and mix.
3. Follow directions on the box for baking. Cool and eat for snack.
4. Send a wrapped piece home with each child with an explanatory note to parents.

Variation/Way to Extend:

- Let the children wear their beads when they sit down to eat their cornbread. Have a feast!

CORNBREAD RECIPE
2 cups corn meal
2 teaspoons baking powder
¾ cup of milk
2 eggs
1 cup cold water
2 tablespoons oil
1 teaspoon salt

Beat eggs and milk together. Stir together corn meal, baking powder, and salt. Add water and mix. Combine egg and milk mixture with dry ingredients and add oil. Stir all until smooth. Pour into 8″ by 8″ baking pan (greased). Bake at 450° for 30 minutes or until golden. Cut into squares and enjoy for a snack.

I-50 NATIVE DRUMS

Subject Areas: Music and Art

Concepts/Skills: Paints with a large brush
Develops rhythmic responsiveness

Objectives: The children will construct and play an Indian drum.

Materials:
- Oatmeal containers
- Masking tape
- Paint
- Paintbrushes

Procedure:

1. Discuss Indians' use of the drum, such as for rituals and signals.
2. Have an oatmeal container for each child. Let the children cover the sides with paint (first tape top in place). Let dry.
3. Demonstrate a simple beat and have the children imitate. Have a child beat on his or her drum one, two, three, or four beats. Ask the children to listen and beat their drums the same number of times. They may choose to get up and move to the beat also.

Variation/Way to Extend:
- Read *Let's Be Indians* by Peggy Parish (New York: Harper & Row, Pub., 1962).

I-51 THANKSGIVING DINNER

Subject Area: Creative Dramatics/Movement

Concepts/Skills: Shows simple symbolic play
Cooperates in a group

Objective: The children will develop an awareness of Thanksgiving Day by pretending to celebrate the holiday with their friends.

Materials: • Props for housekeeping area: tablecloth, centerpiece, dishes, cups, silverware

Procedure:

1. Set out extra props in the housekeeping area to encourage children to think about Thanksgiving.

2. Use artificial fruits and vegetables for them to celebrate a Thanksgiving dinner. Use mounted pictures of turkeys, potatoes, cranberry sauce, pies, and so forth to have plenty for children to use in preparing a feast. (Frozen T.V. dinner boxes are a good source for colorful pictures.) Provide Play-Doh, rolling pins, cookie cutters, and pie pans for "baking" activities.

3. Put out aprons or jackets for dress-up clothes.

Variation/Way to Extend:

• Read the story *Little Bear's Thanksgiving* by Else H. Minarik (New York: Harper & Row, Pub., 1961).

I–52 THANKFUL BOOK

Subject Area: Language Arts

Concepts/Skills: Verbalizes wants
Describes items in two or three words
Applies glue and pastes pieces

Objectives: The children will select representative pictures and paste them into a book.

Materials:
- Magazine pictures of home and family
- Scissors
- 8½″ by 11″ colored construction paper
- Paste
- Markers

Procedure:

1. Discuss the idea of being thankful (saying "thank you," being glad you have something or somebody).
2. Place the pictures of home and family objects, including family members, food, houses, pets, and beds, on a table. Let children select something that they are thankful for.
3. Help them cut around the picture and paste it onto the construction paper. Print on the page "I am thankful for _____."
4. Assemble all the pages together for a class Thankful Book. See if children can identify their page.

Variations/Ways to Extend:

- Use any leftover pictures to make a mural.
- Listen to Hap Palmer's "Things I'm Thankful For" from *Holiday Songs and Rhythms* available from Educational Activities, Inc., Freeport, N.Y. 11520.

I-53 SWEET POTATO PLANTS

Subject Area: Science

Concept/Skill: Associates word with correct object (potato, root, leaves)

Objective: The children will observe the growth of a sweet potato plant.

Materials:
- Sweet potatoes
- Clear plastic cups
- Toothpicks
- Water
- Labels
- Markers

Procedure:

1. Talk about typical Thanksgiving foods.
2. Give each child a sweet potato and discuss its color, texture, shape, and so forth. Discuss that it's an edible part of a plant that can sprout roots and become a lovely green sweet potato plant.
3. Give each child a cup of water filled half full. Help them position toothpicks around the potato so that it will rest half submerged on the edge of the cup.
4. Label each cup with the child's name.
5. Place the cups in sunlight. Observe and transplant them in dirt when strong roots grow.

Variation/Way to Extend:
- Keep a chart to record date roots, shoots, and leaves first appear.

I-54 CANDIED SWEET POTATOES

Subject Area: Nutrition/Foods Experience

Concepts/Skills: Develops a sense of smell and of taste
Spoon feeds without spilling
Understands difference between hard and soft

Objective: The children will participate in making candied sweet potatoes.

Materials:
- Sweet potatoes
- ½ cup brown sugar ⎫
- ¼ cup butter   ⎬ for every six potatoes
- 1 teaspoon salt   ⎭
- Measuring cups
- Spoons
- Peeler
- Knife
- Water
- Saucepan
- Oven or toaster oven
- Baking dish

Procedure:

1. Demonstrate how to peel potatoes. Then peel enough for the class. Point out to the children that the potatoes are hard.

2. Cut the peeled potatoes in quarters and boil in salted water until almost tender. Drain and place them in a baking dish.

3. Measure the butter and brown sugar. Let the children sprinkle the brown sugar over the potatoes and place pats of butter on top.

4. Bake at 375° F in a preheated oven for 30 minutes. (**Caution:** Be sure the children stay away from the hot oven.)

5. When the potatoes are done, let the children savor the smell and then, using spoons, taste the cooled potatoes and eat as a snack.

6. Point out to the children that the sweet potatoes are now soft.

Variations/Ways to Extend:

- Use canned sweet potatoes instead of boiling the potatoes first. This will cut down on preparation time.
- Prepare white potatoes the same way and have the children compare their color and taste with those of the sweet potato.

I–55   THANKSGIVING PLACEMAT

Subject Area: Art

Concepts/Skills: Colors with large crayons
Counts up to ten
Develops new vocabulary words "feathers" and "wattles"

Objective: The children will create placemats for Thanksgiving by tracing their hands and making them into turkeys.

Materials:
- 11″ by 18″ construction paper (light color)
- Black marker
- Crayons

Procedure:

1. Help each child trace his or her hands on the paper with the black marker. Count their fingers.
2. Help them make an eye and a red wattle on each thumb to turn their hand shapes into turkeys. They can color the fingers different colors for feathers.
3. Help them draw stick legs and feet with their black crayons. They can use a green crayon to color grass beneath the turkeys.
4. Write "Happy Thanksgiving" on each placemat and laminate it or cover with clear self-stick vinyl. Let the children make these to take home for Thanksgiving.

Variation/Way to Extend:

- Teach the following rhyme:

    The turkey is a funny bird.
    His head goes wobble, wobble.
    The only sound that he can make
    Is gobble, gobble, gobble.

THE SPIRIT OF THE SEASON

- ○ Giving and Sharing
- ○ Holiday Games
- ○ Children Around the World
- ○ Holiday Foods and Traditions

I-56 HOLIDAY PAINTING

Subject Area: Art

Concepts/Skills: Develops fine motor skills
Applies paint to paper
Glues and pastes

Objective: The children will construct a holiday painting to give to their parents.

Materials:
- Dark green construction paper
- Sprigs of evergreen
- Small aluminum pans
- White tempera paint
- Tissue paper (colored)
- Glue
- Smocks or old shirts

Procedure:

1. Provide each child with a sheet of dark green construction paper, a sprig of evergreen, a small aluminum pan containing a layer of white tempera paint, and a smock.
2. Assist each child in dipping the evergreen sprig into the white paint and spreading it across the green paper.
3. Precut a Christmas tree shape out of green construction paper to be stapled on top of the painted paper.
4. Provide the children with squares of tissues paper to paste under and around the trees for presents.

Variations/Ways to Extend:

- Write a brief note to the parents (you might want to make a master and then duplicate it) explaining that the holiday painting is a gift from the child. Describe the process of making the picture and how well the children enjoyed doing it.
- Read the poem "Christmas Tree" by B. J. Lee, found in *Hello Year,* poems selected by Leland Jacobs (Champaign, Ill.: Garrard Publishing, 1972).

Weekly Subtheme: Giving and Sharing

I-57 AROUND THE TREE

Subject Area: Creative Dramatics/Movement

Concepts/Skills: Imitates actions of adults
Repeats parts of nursery rhyme

Objectives: The children will sing a song and act out the motions.

Materials:
- Christmas tree—model or picture
- Words to the song "Around the Tree"

Procedure:

1. Sing the following to the tune of "Mulberry Bush" while sitting around the tree.
2. Demonstrate each motion so the children can imitate:

> Around the tree the children go,
> Children go, children go.
> Around the tree the children go.
> So early in the morning.
>
> This is the way we trim the tree ...
> This is the way we bounce our ball ...
> This is the way we walk our dolls ...
> See us run our choo-choo trains ...
> This is the way we fly our planes ...
> Jack in the box will jump up high ...
> This is the way we give a gift ...

Variations/Ways to Extend:

- Decorate a large tree and place the actual items to be sung about around the tree.
- Ask a child to pick a toy and show what to do with it. Then have everyone sing and act out the motions.

Weekly Subtheme: Giving and Sharing

I–58 HARD AND SOFT SANTA

Subject Area: Science

Concept/Skill: Understands hard and soft

Objective: The children will learn about hard and soft by creating a Santa face.

Materials:
- Hard and soft items (see list in Procedure section)
- Premade Santa face
- Glue

Procedure:

1. Place the following items on a table: cotton balls, soft sponge, pile of yarn, marshmallows, small walnuts, marbles, and metal caps.
2. Have each child take a turn, first feeling and identifying a hard and soft object. Praise their responses; do not criticize a wrong answer.
3. After everyone has had a turn, give each child a premade Santa Claus face containing only a cut out of his red cap, while the face is left blank.
4. Assist the children in gluing the cotton and other items to create a Santa face: eyes, eyebrows, nose, mouth, and beard.

Variation/Way to Extend:

- Make soft and hard bags and soft and hard books. Allow the children to place and paste soft and hard objects in the bags and on the books.

I-59   GIVE A GIFT

Subject Area: Music

Concepts/Skills: Repeats parts of a song
Acts out a simple story
Claps with music

Objectives: The children will sing a simple melody and clap and ring bells to the tune.

Materials: • Words to the song "Give, Give, Give a Gift"
• Jingle bells to shake
• One large, wrapped gift

Procedure:

1. Sing the following song to the children (tune of "Row, Row, Row Your Boat"):

   Give, give, give a gift,
   At Christmas time this year.
   Merrily, merrily, merrily, merrily,
   We share our Christmas cheer.

2. Clap your hands to the beat and ask the children to clap with you.
3. Repeat the words with them and have them sing it with you.
4. Give out the jingle bells and have them clap their hands with the bells to the beat.
5. Have two children act out the song by giving a gift from one to the other as it's sung.

Variations/Ways to Extend:

• Have the children make holiday cards.
• Do the same activity with a holiday card. Sing instead: "Send, send, send a card," and so forth.

I-60   GIFT BOOK

Subject Area: Language Arts

Concepts/Skills: Turns single pages
Refers to self by name
Uses short sentences to convey simple idea

Objective: The children will make a holiday book to give as a gift.

Materials: • Heavy stock 8½" by 11" paper
• Notebook rings
• Hole puncher
• Old Christmas cards
• Glue

Procedure:

1. Use heavy stock paper to make a book for each child. Place the paper horizontally and punch two holes on the left side. Use small notebook rings purchased from stationery stores to bind the books.
2. On an individual basis, sit with each child and talk about making the book. Encourage the child to say his or her name and show how you write it on the front cover of the book.
3. Let the child turn to the first page and mark ownership by making a few lines or mandalas (circles) with a crayon. Demonstrate if necessary.
4. Using the pictures of Christmas scenes from the old cards, let each child choose several for his or her book.
5. Let them paste one on each page, with you writing a one- or two-word description given by the child.

Variation/Way to Extend:

• Read *Christmas Fun Book* by Patti Carson and Janet Dellosa (Akron, Ohio: Carson-Delosa, 1981).

Weekly Subtheme: Holiday Games

I-61 HOLIDAY COLORS

Subject Areas: Science and Language Arts

Concepts/Skills: Matches color samples
Distinguishes between red and green

Objective: The children will be able to distinguish between red and green.

Materials: • Red and green holiday items (ribbons, bows, candles, ornaments, glitter, evergreen twigs, and holly wreaths)

Procedure:

1. Identify each of the holiday items and emphasize the red or green color of each.
2. Let the children explore the objects by touching and smelling each one.
3. Place two items at a time in front of the children and ask, "Who can point to the red ?" "Who can point to the green ?"
4. Taking turns, let the children identify the correct color for each object.
5. Then point to each item and ask, "What color is this?"

Variation/Way to Extend:

• Provide paper and glue and allow each child to create either a collage of red objects or a collage of green objects. Have a supply of magazine pictures handy for the children to select.

Weekly Subtheme: Holiday Games

I-62 HOLIDAY HEADBANDS

Subject Areas: Art and Music

Concepts/Skills: Applies glue
Claps along with music

Objectives: The children will be able to construct a holiday headband and dance along to holiday music.

Materials:
- Green construction paper
- Recording of "Jingle Bells"
- Scissors
- Glue
- Glitter
- Large gold stars
- Cellophane tape

Procedure:

1. Using green construction paper, cut a Christmas tree for each child. Then measure each child's head with a strip of construction paper and tape the ends together for the headband.
2. Help each child glue the tree to the headband.
3. Help each child spread glue onto the tree and headband and then sprinkle glitter onto the glued areas.
4. Let the children lick the gold stars and attach them to the headbands.

5. Play "Jingle Bells" and encourage the children to dance and clap along with the music while wearing their holiday headbands.

Variation/Way to Extend:

- Read one of the holiday fingerplays in *Let's Do Fingerplays* by Marion Grayson (Bridgeport, Conn.: Luce, 1962).

I-63 POP-UP

Subject Area: Language Arts

Concepts/Skills: Follows simple rules
Repeats part of a rhyme
Develops gross motor movement of jumping

Objectives: The children will be able to participate in a game and repeat a rhyme.

Materials: • Words to the rhyme (see Procedure section)
• Decorated cardboard box

Procedure:

1. Decorate a large cardboard box like a present. Keep the lid attached.
2. Cut off one entire side for the children to enter and exit. Be sure the box is large enough for a two-year-old to fit into.

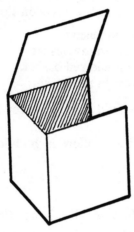

3. Play "Pop-Up" by having each child take a turn climbing into the box with the lid closed. (The open side should not face the other children.)
4. Ask the other children to sing the following rhyme (sung to the tune of "Twinkle, Twinkle Little Star"):

> Open, open, come and play
> You can hide another day.
> Can you smile, can you hop?
> Can you open up and pop?
> Open, open, come and play
> You can hide another day!

5. At the end of the rhyme, have the child inside the box pop up like a jack-in-the-box.

Variations/Ways to Extend:

• Place several cardboard boxes of varying sizes in the classroom to encourage gross motor and symbolic play. Develop the concepts of inside and outside.
• Obtain the 11″ by 14″ color reproduction entitled "Hide and Seek" (No. 2729) by James Jacques Tissot, available from National Gallery of Art, Publication Service, Washington, D.C. 20565. Write for current prices and any handling charges.
• Teach the children a simple version of hide-and-seek.

I-64 RED AND GREEN BASKET

Subject Area: Gross Motor Games

Concepts/Skills: Walks on tiptoe
Recognizes red and green

Objectives: The children will be able to participate in a game, recognizing red and green colors.

Materials:
- Cardboard boxes
- Red and green paper
- Basket

Procedure:

1. Decorate two small cardboard boxes (4″ to 6″ long) using green and red paper.
2. Place the children in a circle.
3. Give one child who is sitting the red decorated box. Ask another child to take a basket (decorate in green and red) and walk around the circle on tiptoe while the children sing:

   A tisket, a tasket, a green and red basket.
   I found a little red gift and put it in my basket.
   My basket, my basket, my green and red basket.
   I found a little red gift and put it in my basket.

4. When the song is completed, ask the child holding the red gift to give it to the child with the basket.
5. Repeat, using the green gift as well, and allow each child a turn holding the gift and the basket.

Variation/Way to Extend:

- Use different colors (for example, white or yellow) each time the game is played.

I-65 HOLIDAY PRETEND COOKIES

Subject Area: Creative Dramatics/Movement

Concept/Skill: Imitates actions

Objective: The children will be able to pretend to make holiday cookies using a variety of props.

Materials:
- Flour dough
- Cardboard box
- Small rolling pin
- Cookie cutters
- Cookie sheet or piece of heavy cardboard
- Timer

Procedure:

1. Tell the children they are going to make holiday pretend cookies.
2. Provide small pieces of flour dough and demonstrate how to use a rolling pin and cookie cutters to create cookie shapes.
3. Assist each child in rolling out a piece of flour dough.
4. Place the cookies on a cookie sheet (or heavy cardboard).
5. Put the cookie sheet into the "oven," a cardboard box with a cut flap that can be opened and closed as an oven door.

6. Pretend to turn on the heat. Use a timer and set for 5 minutes.
7. While the children are waiting for their "cookies" to be "done," remind them that they are making pretend cookies. After they have washed their hands, distribute real holiday cookies and milk for a snack.
8. Ask the children to remind you when the timer sounds so the pretend cookies can be taken out of the "oven."

Variations/Ways to Extend:
- Paint the cardboard box to look like a real stove.
- Pretend to cook and bake other foods using flour dough.

I-66   LISTEN AND PLAY

Subject Area: Music

Concepts/Skills: Participates with pleasure
Distinguishes between loud and soft, fast and slow

Objectives: The children will accompany musical selections with instruments.

Materials: • Rhythm instruments, such as bells, clappers, triangle, and sand blocks.
• Music of other countries (several albums available through U.S. Committee for UNICEF, 331 East 38th Street, New York, NY 10016)

Procedure:

1. Let the children experiment with the instruments. Help them find ways to hold and move the instruments to produce pleasing sounds.
2. Play the recordings, and have the children practice starting and stopping together.
3. Point out loud and soft parts of the music, and have the children play their instruments accordingly. Try fast and slow as well.

Variation/Way to Extend:

• Bells may be sewn on elastic and worn on ankles or wrists. The children can also march while they play.

I-67   CHINESE FANS

Subject Area: Art

Concept/Skill: Applies glue

Objective: The children will create Chinese fan decorations.

Materials:
- Styrofoam meat trays
- Scissors
- Tongue depressors
- Cellophane tape
- Pink tissue paper
- Glue

Procedure:

1. Cut oval fan shapes from the styrofoam meat trays and tape tongue depressors to the backs. Make one for each child.
2. Help the children apply glue to the fans and decorate with pink tissue paper.
3. Tell the children that in China, ornamental fans are used as decorations.

Variation/Way to Extend:

- Sing the following variation of "If You're Happy and You Know It":
     If you're happy and you know it, wave your fan (*teacher claps twice*).
     If you're happy and you know it, wave your fan (*teacher claps twice*).
     If you're happy and you know it, then wave your fan to show it.
     If you're happy and you know it, wave your fan (*teacher claps twice*).

I-68   PIÑATA SEARCH

Subject Area: Language Arts

Concept/Skill: Follows simple rules

Objectives: The children will participate in a game and observe the teacher break the piñata.

Materials:
- Grocery bags
- Scissors
- Aluminum foil
- Colored tissue paper
- Blindfold
- String
- Stick
- Small paper cups
- Twin-sized sheet
- Wrapped candies; uninflated balloons; and small, inexpensive toys

Procedure:

1. Make several simple Mexican piñatas by decorating grocery bags, as shown here. Draw a picture of an animal on each bag and decorate with aluminium foil and colored tissue paper.

2. Fill each bag with wrapped candies, uninflated balloons, and small inexpensive toys.
3. Show the children the piñatas and explain that youngsters in Mexico play a game with the piñatas. Ask, "Would you like to play a game, too?"
4. Have the children close their eyes while you hide each piñata in locations within the room that are accessible to the children.
5. Tell the children to open their eyes and look for the piñatas. Assist them if they need help.
6. Once they find all the piñatas, demonstrate the game that Mexican children play, usually around Christmas.
7. Ask the children to sit around a sheet.
8. Attach the piñata to a string hanging from the ceiling, directly above the sheet.
9. With your shoes off and while holding a small stick, place a blindfold over your eyes and explain that you are going to try and hit the piñata with the stick.
10. Turn yourself around several times and purposely move away from the piñata, asking the children for help.
11. Finally, find the piñata and break it open with the stick, allowing the "goodies" to fall onto the sheet.
12. Ask each child to remain seated around the sheet while you give each one a small paper cup. Place one piece of wrapped candy, one uninflated balloon, and one small toy in each cup.

Variation/Way to Extend:

- Gather the children in a circle. Using other piñatas hung from the ceiling with a string, have one child at a time stand before it without a blindfold. As you turn the child around, everyone sings, "Round, round, turn around, hit the piñata to the ground." Let the child take one swing (no sticks used) at the piñata. Repeat the song with each child. When finished, take the piñata down, and let the children enjoy the contents.

I-69 FRENCH HOLIDAY MEAL

Subject Area: Nutrition/Foods Experience

Concepts/Skills: Describes what happens in two or three words
Mixes ingredients
Learns vocabulary words about cooking

Objective: The children will assist in making pancakes.

Materials: • Electric frypan
• Ingredients for pancakes

Procedure:

1. In France, families celebrate Christmas day with one of several types of meals: goose, oysters, turkey, or buckwheat cakes and sour cream.
2. Assist the children in making pancakes.
3. Use boxed pancake mix and follow ingredients and directions given. (Or prepare batter from scratch.)
4. Cook in a lightly buttered electric frypan and serve with honey or syrup. (**Caution:** Be sure the children stay away from the hot frypan.)
5. As each ingredient is measured, identify the ingredient and ask the children to repeat the name.
6. Encourage the children to use words such as "mix," "beat," "stir," and "bake."

Variation/Way to Extend:

• For additional snacks, mix yogurt and crushed fruit or low-sugar jelly in a bowl and serve. Note the color change.

I–70 LET'S GO AROUND THE WORLD

Subject Area: Social Studies

Concepts/Skills: Repeats parts of a song
Follows directions
Explores new materials
Paints with a large brush
Shows simple symbolic play

Objectives: The children will be able to pretend they are on a train and sing a song.

Materials:
- Words to song "The Wheels on the Train Go 'Round and 'Round"
- Cardboard boxes
- Hole puncher
- 1″ by 2″ strips of paper

Procedure:

1. Invite the children to go on a pretend train ride to visit children from around the world. Remind the children of the previous lessons involving Chinese, Mexican, and French children. You might want to show the children pictures of trains.

2. Gather enough cardboard boxes so that two children sit on each one. Line up the boxes in two rows to resemble train seats.

3. Give each child a strip of paper to be collected as tickets. Explain that they cannot board the train without a ticket. (When checking the tickets, punch each one with a hole puncher.)

4. When the children are seated, begin the trip by singing the following song to the tune of "The Wheels on the Bus Go 'Round and 'Round":

    The wheels on the train
    Go 'round and round (*turn hands around each other*)
    'Round and 'round,
    'Round and 'round.
    The wheels on the train
    Go 'round and 'round
    All over town.

5. Encourage the children to pretend there are Chinese, Mexican, and French children waving to them, so ask them to wave back as the train passes through each country.

Variation/Way to Extend:

- After the train ride, guide the children to art easels and talk about painting a picture of a train. Allow the children to freely express themselves at the easels, realizing that two-year-olds are not capable of truly representational art yet. Be sure to praise their efforts. While the paint is still wet, assist each child in placing large circles of colored tissue paper onto the painting. Explain that the circles are the wheels of the train.

I-71   HOLIDAY AROMAS

Subject Area: Thinking Game

Concepts/Skills: Develops senses of touch, smell, and taste
Learns to pour and mix

Objectives: The children will use their senses to identify holiday aromas and make a holiday punch.

Materials:
- Book
- Ingredients for punch } see Procedure section
- Saucepan
- Stove or burner

Procedure:

1. Read and paraphrase parts of *The Sweet Smell of Christmas* by Patricia M. Scarry (New York: Western, 1970) to the children. This is a scratch-and-sniff book featuring the scents of apple pie, pine tree, candy cane, gingerbread, hot chocolate, and orange.
2. Allow the children to take turns scratching and sniffing the different scents.
3. Assist the children in identifying the name of the food or item associated with each smell.
4. Make a holiday punch from the following ingredients:

   1 quart of cranberry juice
   2 sticks of cinnamon
   6 cloves
   1 cup of orange juice
   1 cup of lemon juice

   Slowly heat the cranberry juice along with the cinnamon and cloves for approximately 10 minutes. (**Caution:** Be sure the children stay away from the heat.) Remove the cinnamon and cloves and add the fruit juices. Serve warm, having allowed the children to take turns smelling, pouring, and mixing.

Variation/Way to Extend:

- Serve peeled and sliced apples during snack time, and encourage the children to recall the scent of apple pie from the Scarry book.

I-72 HOLIDAY PICTURES

Subject Area: Language Arts

Concept/Skill: Names pictured objects

Objective: The children will be able to identify objects in the pictures presented.

Materials: • Pictures of holiday items

Procedure:

1. Show the children simple pictures of holiday traditions, such as presents, evergreen trees, decorations, wreaths, and bells. Show each picture one at a time.
2. Ask such questions as, "Who can find the Christmas tree in this picture?"
3. Where possible, associate the real object with the picture.

Variations/Ways to Extend:

• Emphasize the colors red and green.
• Read *A Christmas Story* by Mary Chalmers (New York: Harper & Row, Pub., 1971).

I–73   REINDEER COOKIES

Subject Area: Nutrition/Foods Experience

Concepts/Skills: Names pictured objects
Uses cookie cutter
Learns to mix dough

Objectives: The children will identify reindeer and make reindeer cookies.

Materials: • Pictures of Santa Claus, his sleigh, and reindeer
• Ingredients for cookies
• Cookie cutters
• Pastry board
• Rolling pin
• Wax paper
• Cookie sheet
• Oven
• Milk

Procedure:

1. Show pictures of Santa's sleigh and his reindeer. Help the children to identify what's in the picture.
2. Make reindeer cookies by following the recipe:

   Mix ½ cup of brown sugar with 1 stick of softened butter or margarine.
   Add 1 cup of flour and 3 drops of vanilla.
   Allow the children to mix the dough.
   Mold into a ball and roll out on a floured board under a piece of wax paper.
   Assist the children in cutting out reindeer-shaped cookies.
   Bake on a cookie sheet at 300° F for 6 to 8 minutes.
   (**Caution:** Be sure the children stay away from the oven.)

3. Serve the cookies with milk.

Variation/Way to Extend:

• Let the children listen to the song "Rudolph, the Red-Nosed Reindeer" while they enjoy their cookies and milk.

Weekly Subtheme: Holiday Foods and Traditions

I–74   SPONGE PAINT DECORATIONS

Subject Area: Art

Concept/Skill: Differentiates circle and square

Objective: The children will create decorations for their Christmas trees.

Materials: • Green construction paper cut into Christmas tree shapes.
- Paint shirt and newspaper
- Styrofoam meat trays or other containers for paint
- Red, white, and yellow tempera paint
- Sponges cut into circles and squares

Procedure:

1. Place a Christmas tree on a table in front of each child.
2. Pour red, white, and yellow tempera paint into separated styrofoam meat trays.
3. Dip sponges (cut into circles and squares) into paint (different sponges for each color).
4. Squeeze extra paint from sponge.
5. Assist each child in pressing different colored sponges onto the Christmas tree.
6. Point to round- and square-shaped decorations. Encourage each child to identify circles and squares.

Variation/Way to Extend:

- Glue the Christmas tree on a piece of dark blue construction paper. Use white tempera paint and small sponges to create snowflakes around the tree.

I–75   PRETEND SANTA

Subject Area: Creative Dramatics/Movement

Concept/Skill: Acts out a simple routine

Objectives: The children will decorate a tree and pretend it is the night that Santa is coming.

Materials:
- Pictures of Santa Claus
- Precut decorations
- Crayons
- Blankets
- Cookies and milk
- Pillows
- Gift boxes, wrapped
- Small toys
- Record (see Procedure section)

Procedure:

1. Show pictures of Santa Claus riding on his sleigh, climbing down chimneys, and so forth.
2. Precut simple tree decorations in shape of balls, trees, candy canes, and stockings. Place a paper clip through the top of each as a hook.
3. Allow the children to color the decorations with crayons and decorate a small evergreen tree.
4. Have each child place a cookie on the table for Santa to eat.
5. Give the children blankets and pillows. Tell them to pretend to be asleep.
6. Pretend to be Santa (wear a hat or beard) and leave presents under the tree.
7. The presents can be small cardboard boxes with lids separately gift wrapped so they can be opened without damaging the wrapping. Inside each box can be either a cookie or a small toy for each child. (All boxes should contain identical gifts.)
8. Have the children "wake up" and open their presents.
9. Let the children enjoy the cookies and milk.
10. Sing or listen to the record "Santa Claus is Coming to Town."

Variation/Way to Extend:

- Let the children help you make and drink eggnog. The following recipe makes enough for two children, so increase the measurements accordingly: In a blender, mix 1 beaten egg, ½ teaspoon sugar, ⅛ teaspoon vanilla, a pinch of salt, ¼ cup milk, and 1 scoop vanilla ice cream. Blend for several seconds until smooth.

WINTER

○ Getting a Fresh Start

○ Health and Safety

○ Snow

○ Water and Ice

Weekly Subtheme: Getting a Fresh Start

I–76 SOMETHING NEW TO DO

Subject Area: Thinking Games

Concepts/Skills: Follows simple directions
Understands idea of waiting for someone else to go first

Objective: The children will demonstrate desirable two-year-old skills.

Materials:
- Fish cut from white tagboard, approximately 4″ by 6″
- Pictures of children demonstrating desirable behaviors (glue pictures onto fish)
- String
- Magnets
- Dowels

Procedure:

1. Discuss the idea that a new year is beginning and we should look forward to learning how to do new things.
2. Show the fish and explain the pictures, which might include children looking at books, eating unassisted, walking up or down stairs, or building a block tower. (Refer to the Skills-Concepts Checklist for more ideas.)
3. Attach one end of the string to the dowel and a magnet to the other end.
4. Have each child take a turn fishing for a picture.
5. Describe the action in the picture, and assist the child in demonstrating a specific skill.
6. Allow each child to fish about four times.

Variations/Ways to Extend:

- Cut out from magazines additional pictures of children riding a horse, swimming, jumping, playing ball, and so forth. Let the children create a collage with these pictures
- Assist the children in painting the fish (made of white tagboard), and have them play a game of matching colors.

I–77   NEW FOODS FOR THE NEW YEAR

Subject Area: Nutrition/Foods Experience

Concepts/Skills: Labels foods
Develops sensory awareness
Understands concepts of part and whole

Objectives: The children will sample some fruits and vegetables and identify them.

Materials: • Fresh fruits and vegetables both whole and cut up
• Plates

Procedure:

1. Introduce the various fruits and vegetables by talking about color, size, shape, texture, and aroma. Talk about how important fresh foods are in keeping us healthy and growing.
2. Place several fruits and vegetables on a plate, and allow the children to make selections to eat. Have them try to recall the names of each food from what you told them earlier.
3. Prepare one plate of whole fruits and vegetables and another plate with the same produce cut into pieces. Discuss the ideas of part and whole.

Variation/Way to Extend:

• Have the children take turns matching cut-up pieces to the whole fruit or vegetable.

I-78 BIRTHDAY TREE

Subject Area: Social Studies

Concepts/Skills: Understands concept of birthday
Identifies own gender
Knows colors of pink and blue

Objectives: The children will identify their gender and place a leaf with their birthdate on a tree.

Materials:
• Tree shape cut from paper with twelve branches
• Cellophane Tape
• Leaf shapes (pink for girls, blue for boys) with each child's name and birthdate

Procedure:

1. Display the tree. Explain that it is winter so the branches are bare, but the children can put pretty birthday leaves on the tree to fill it up.
2. Ask each child if they are a girl or a boy, and tell the children which color pile to look in for their leaf.
3. Help the children find their particular leaf and match it to the appropriate month on the tree. Tape the leaves to the tree.
4. Sing "Happy Birthday to Us" when all the leaves are on the tree.

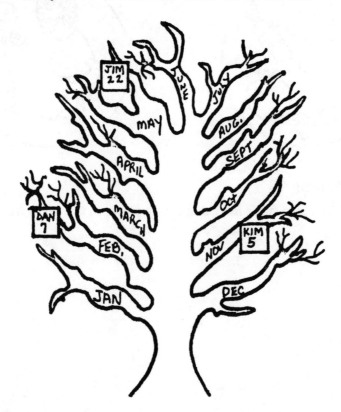

Variation/Way to Extend:

• Cut out a birthday cake with candles containing name and birthdate information.

I-79   NEW YEAR POEM

Subject Area: Math

Concepts/Skills: Counts to two
Indicates awareness of more than two

Objectives: The children will listen for a word and demonstrate it by holding up fingers.

Materials: • Words to the poem (see Procedure section)
• Number cards or objects

Procedure:

1. Discuss how old the children are now. Many will be two. Ask them to hold up two of their fingers to show two.
2. Explain that sometime soon many will have a birthday and become three. Have them hold up three fingers.
3. Find examples of three of a kind in the room.
4. Recite the poem and have children hold up three fingers when they hear the word three.

> It's the new year
> How old will you be?
> OK, let's see
> One, two, three (*hold up fingers*)
> That's right, you'll be three.

Variation/Way to Extend:

• Recite another rhyme:
> One, two, three (*hold up fingers, one at a time*)
> Look at me (*point to self*)!
> One, two, three (*hold up fingers, one at a time*)
> I'll be three (*hold up three fingers*)!

Weekly Subtheme: Getting a Fresh Start

1-80 SOMETHING OLD, SOMETHING NEW

Subject Area: Language Arts

Concepts/Skills: Groups things together
Names common objects

Objectives: The children will distinguish between objects that are old and new and match an old item to a new one.

Materials:
- Two sets of objects that are the same except that one is old and one is new (shoes, sneakers, pencils, items of clothing that show wear, toys)
- Two calendars, one new and one old
- Large box
- Table

Procedure:

1. Show the children the objects, and discuss which are old and which are new.
2. Explain the calendars. Say, "A calendar helps us keep track of days. This square (point to it) was for yesterday. This square (point to it) is for today. Can you tell which square stands for tomorrow?"
3. Play a game by separating the old and new items. Place the old ones in a large box and the new ones on a table.
4. Let each child, in turn, go to the box and pick out an old item. Ask the child to identify the object and then go to the table and find the similar object that is new.
5. Emphasize that we are starting a new year when the old calendar is matched with the new one.

Variations/Ways to Extend:

- Play the game using simple picture cards of old and new pairs of objects.
- Make puzzle pieces of old and new pictures that can be paired by interlocking shapes.

I–81   CLEAN AND HEALTHY

Subject Area: Creative Dramatics/Movement

Concepts/Skills: Associates use with common objects
Repeats parts of rhyme
Begins to understand cleanliness

Objective: The children will act out a fingerplay about keeping clean and healthy.

Materials: • Words to the fingerplay (see Procedure section)
• Display items: comb and brush; toothbrush and toothpaste; soap, washcloth, and towel; and so forth

Procedure:

1. Display items and discuss how they are used to keep us clean.
2. Have the children sit on the floor so they can see you well.
3. Demonstrate the action rhyme using a pretend comb, and so forth. Ask the children to join you in making the actions.

> I comb my hair,
> I brush my teeth,
> I wash myself
> Down to my feet.
> I eat what's right,
> Get my sleep at night,
> So I'll feel good
> Just as I should.

Variation/Way to Extend:

• Place the items in a bag and have the children take turns reaching in, feeling an object, and acting out how to use it. Ask the other children to guess what is being done.

I-82   WEATHER WILLIE (OR WANDA)

Subject Area: Science

Concepts/Skills: Begins to understand hot and cold
Puts on and removes coat unassisted
Counts to two

Objective: The children will identify clothing worn to protect our bodies from the cold.

Materials: • Flannelboard figure (see pattern)
• Appropriate felt- or flannel-backed pictures of winter clothing

Procedure:

1. Discuss winter. "Is it hot or cold?" "What should we wear to keep warm?" "What happens if we don't dress properly?" (We might catch a cold or get an earache, for example.)
2. Tell the children that they're going to dress Weather Willie (or Wanda) for a winter day. You might want to explain that some people live in warm climates even in winter, so winter clothing would not be necessary.
3. Ask for suggestions after displaying the possible clothing. Have the children identify the clothing and tell where each piece is worn.
4. Let the children put the clothes on Willie (or Wanda).
5. Discuss what a *pair* means—two mittens, shoes, boots, and so forth.
6. Have the children find a pair of mittens, a pair of rubbers, and so forth in the clothes closet. Let them try to put on their mittens, boots, and coats without help.

Variations/Ways to Extend:

• Have the children put their outer clothing in a pile and practice dressing for a cold, winter day. Ask the children to tell you the clothing's name as they put on each piece.
• Provide Willie (or Wanda) with some items that are not appropriate (swimsuit, sunglasses) for winter, unless, of course, you live in a warm climate.

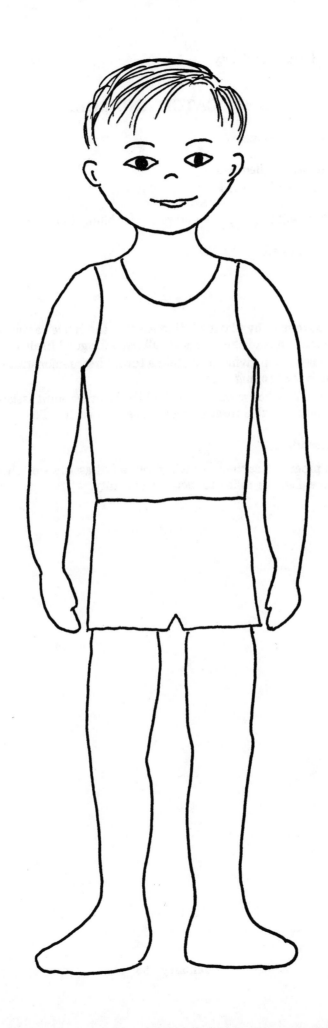

Weekly Subtheme: Health and Safety

I-83 CATCH AND ROLL

Subject Area: Gross Motor Games

Concepts/Skills: Catches a rolled ball
Rolls a ball forward

Objectives: The children will play a game and practice rolling and catching a ball.

Materials:
- Large rubber ball
- Open area

Procedure:

1. Warm up for movement by playing "Ring Around the Rosie" a few times. Explain to children that exercise is one of the things we all need for good health.
2. Two adults are needed in giving each child a turn. First, demonstrate rolling the ball to the other, catching it, and rolling it back.
3. Have one adult roll the ball toward a child while the other adult assists the child in catching and rolling it back. Try this three or four times with each child.

Variation/Way to Extend:

- As the children progress, let them try it without adult assistance. Then vary the size of the ball as well as the distance rolled to increase difficulty.

I-84 SAFETY SALLY

Subject Area: Social Studies

Concepts/Skills: Begins to distinguish between safe and unsafe
Helps put things away

Objectives: The children will listen to a puppet talk about toy safety and apply what they've learned to cleaning up.

Materials:
- Safety Sally puppet
- Small toys
- Carpet squares
- Shoe box
- Material
- Needle and thread
- Pinking shears
- Markers or material scraps

Procedure:

1. Make a simple hand puppet from two pieces of material cut with pinking shears and sewn around three sides (see pattern on next page). Use fine-tipped markers or felt scraps and yarn to form the face and hair.
2. Introduce Safety Sally at a time when the room needs cleaning up. Make a miniroom for Sally by placing small toys on a carpet square and having a small shoe box serve as a toy chest.
3. Let the children know that Sally is upset about the mess in her room because she is worried about someone getting hurt by falling and also that the toys may get broken.
4. Talk about places where scattered toys are particularly dangerous, such as on stairs, on the driveway, or in a doorway.
5. Have Sally happily pick up the toys and put them in her toy box. Then let Sally ask the children to clean up and put all their things where they belong.

Variation/Way to Extend:

- Read *Max's Toys: A Counting Book* by Rosemary Wells (New York: Dial Books for Young Readers, 1979).

I-85 WHAT FOODS ARE GOOD AND HEALTHFUL?

Subject Area: Nutrition/Foods Experience

Concepts/Skills: Names common foods
Groups things together
Learns colors

Objective: The children will recall basic foods.

Materials:
- Magazine pictures of foods from the four basic food groups that are known to most two-year-olds, such as fruits and vegetables; bread and grains; meat; cheese and milk.
- Construction paper
- Scissors
- Rubber cement

Procedure:

1. Cut out the magazine pictures of basic foods and mount them on construction paper in advance of the lesson.
2. Explain that some foods are good for us and we need to eat them so we can be strong and feel good.
3. Hold up the pictures of the basic foods and ask the children to identify them. Have the children note the color of the different foods.
4. Have enough pictures available so that each child can hold one once it is identified.
5. After all the pictures have been identified, ask for the pictures back, one by one, saying, "Who has the picture of the eggs?" and so on.

Variations/Ways to Extend:

- Mount duplicate pictures of basic foods and ask the children to match them.
- Play "Picture Memory." Display two different pictures of basic foods at a time. After identifying them, ask the children to close their eyes. Remove one picture and have the children guess which one is missing.
- Bring in some foods from the basic groups and let the children enjoy sampling them.

I-86   SNOW PICTURE

Subject Area: Art

Concepts/Skills: Expresses creatively
Uses new materials

Objective: The children will create a snowlike picture using salt.

Materials:
- Blue construction paper
- White tempera paint
- Watered glue
- Salt in large shakers
- Paintbrushes

Procedure:

1. Allow the children to freely paint white tempera onto blue construction paper. Let dry.
2. Have the students brush some watered glue over the dry tempera.
3. Help the children to sprinkle salt over the glued areas. After tipping off the excess, allow the glue to dry thoroughly.
4. Display the finished snow pictures.

Variation/Way to Extend:

- Read *The Snow* by John Burningham (New York: Harper & Row, Pub., 1975).

I-87 FALLING SNOW

Subject Area: Language Arts

Concept/Skill: Distinguishes rhyming sounds

Objective: The children will repeat a new fingerplay as a group activity.

Materials:
- Pictures of falling snow
- Slides of snow scenes
- Words to fingerplay (see Procedure section)

Procedure:

1. Show pictures or slides and discuss snowy weather.
2. Demonstrate the following fingerplay:

   Snow, snow
   Falling down (*move hands, like falling snow*).
   Quietly, quietly (*move finger to mouth—sh!*)
   It covers the ground (*move hands back and forth and smooth*).

3. Repeat, asking children to join in.

Variation/Way to Extend:

- Repeat the fingerplay while holding paper snowflakes and letting them fall to the floor at the end.

I-88 EXPLORING SNOW

Subject Area: Science

Concepts/Skills: Develops sense of touch
Observes details

Objectives: The children will examine and draw conclusions about snow.

Materials:
- Black construction paper
- Magnifying glass
- Plastic bowls
- Snow (*hint:* Freeze some snow in advance, if necessary, to be ready for this lesson)

Procedure:

1. On a snowy day, put a piece of black construction paper on an outside window ledge to catch some snowflakes.
2. Allow the children to quickly examine the flakes with a magnifying glass.
3. Explain that each snowflake is different and that each has a different design or shape.
4. Collect more snow to examine and explore. What color is it? How does it feel?
5. Place differing amounts of snow in plastic bowls around the room, such as near the window or by a heat source, and experiment with rates of melting. Where does the snow melt faster?
6. Let the children observe that the result of melting is water. Measure and compare the amounts of water.

Variation/Way to Extend:

- Read *When Will It Snow?* by Syd Hoff (New York: Harper & Row, Pub., 1971).

Weekly Subtheme: Snow

I-89 SNOWMAN COOKIES

Subject Area: Nutrition/Foods Experience

Concepts/Skills: Develops fine motor skills of measuring, mixing, pouring, rolling, and cutting
Develops sense of taste and smell

Objectives: The children will make and bake cookies in the shape of snowmen.

Materials:
- Cookie mix (or dough prepared by the teacher)
- Cookie cutters
- White icing
- Raisins and chocolate or carob chips

Procedure:

1. Using a simple basic butter cookie mix (or prepared dough), make and bake cookies with the children. Have them assist in measuring, mixing, and pouring the ingredients as well as rolling and cutting the dough into circles with cookie cutters.
2. Line up the dough circles to form snowmen shapes on the baking sheets, and follow baking directions.
3. While still warm, decorate snow people with icing, raisins, and chips.

Variations/Ways to Extend:

- Listen to a recording of "Frosty, the Snowman," available from AA Records, 250 West 57th Street, New York, New York 10019.
- A beautiful, big picture book for two-year-olds is *Frosty the Snowman,* retold by Anne N. Bedford (Racine, Wis.: Golden Press, 1979).

Weekly Subtheme: Snow

I–90 SNOW ON THE ROOF

Subject Area: Art and Social Studies

Concepts/Skills: Explores new materials
Develops coordination of hands and eyes

Objective: The children will create snow pictures from various media.

Materials:
- Paper
- Chalk
- Water
- Glue
- Cotton balls

Procedure:

1. Give each child a piece of paper with the shape of a house drawn on it.
2. Have them dip a piece of chalk in the water and color the house. Observe the darker color of the wet chalk and the smoother feel.
3. Dip cotton balls into glue and paste on the rooftop and along the ground for snow.
4. Show them how to align three cotton balls vertically to make snowmen alongside the house.

Variation/Way to Extend:

- Read the Caldecott Medal book *The Snowy Day* by Ezra Jack Keats (New York: Viking, 1972).

I-91 WINTER SCENE

Subject Area: Art

Concepts/Skills: Expresses creatively
Explores new materials
Paints with large brush

Objective: The children will create winter pictures using watercolors.

Materials:
- 9″ by 12″ sheet of white construction paper for each child
- Blue watercolors
- Paintbrushes, large
- Paper cups
- Glue
- Water
- Permanent marker
- Aluminum foil cut in a pond shape (one for each child)

Procedure:

1. Demonstrate and discuss mixing water with paint.
2. Tell the children to mix water with the blue paint and to paint their paper blue.
3. When the papers are dry, give each child a silver pond to glue onto the blue water.
4. Tell the children that the foil stands for some of the water that has frozen and turned into ice.
5. Label the blue water and the foil ice with the permanent marker.

Variation/Way to Extend:

- Mix soap flakes with water and beat lightly. Spoon the mixture onto the picture in piles to represent snow on the ice or at the water's edge.

I-92   SNOWY GELATIN

Subject Area: Math

Concepts/Skills: Develops awareness of more than "two"
Begins to understand hot and cold
Measures and mixes

Objectives: The children will use water to make gelatin and count the marshmallows as they put them into their individual cups.

Materials:
- Boiling water
- Cold water
- Large package of fruit-flavored gelatin (any color you would like to stress)
- Package of miniature marshmallows
- Styrofoam cups with name of each child printed on a different one
- Measuring cup
- Saucepan
- Bowl
- Spoons

Procedure:

1. Pour the gelatin into a bowl. Discuss its color and form with the children.
2. Add boiling water to the gelatin after letting the children watch you pour the hot water and measure two cups. (**Caution:** Be sure the children stay away from the boiling water.) Discuss "hot" and the uses for hot water, such as cooking and washing.
3. Measure 2 cups of cold water. Let the children feel the outside of the cup before pouring it into the gelatin.
4. Distribute the styrofoam cups to the children. Pour ½ cup of gelatin into the individual cups.
5. Let each child add marshmallows to his or her own gelatin cup, counting as he or she puts them in.
6. Let the gelatin harden in a refrigerator or in a safe place outside if it's cold enough. Then enjoy the gelatin as a snack.

Variation/Way to Extend:

- Pour the gelatin mixture into a lipped cookie sheet instead of in individual cups. Refrigerate. When the gelatin is solid, cut it into cubes and let the children enjoy the "wiggly" treat.

I-93   THIS IS THE WAY...

Subject Area: Music

Concepts/Skills: Associates use with common objects
Names common objects
Begins to understand cleanliness
Imitates actions of adults

Objectives: The children will sing the "This Is the Way" song as they act out ways we use water to keep clean and neat.

Materials: • Tune to the song "This Is the Way"
• Display objects: water, soap, washcloth, towel, toothbrush, cup, scrub brush, mop, and rag

Procedure:

1. Display the objects listed above.
2. Let the children guess how they're used and demonstrate on toys or objects.
3. Sing "This is the way we wash our hands," and act out what is done. Do the same for the following: wash our face, bodies, teeth, car, scrub the floor, wall, and so forth. Have the children join in as you sing.

Variations/Ways to Extend:

• Place the objects in a box to take out one by one. Then sing appropriate words to "This Is the Way."
• Play "What's Missing" by putting two of the cleaning objects on display and then hiding one while no one's looking.

I-94 GRAPE FROST

Subject Area: Nutrition/Foods Experience and Science

Concepts/Skills: Develops awareness
Develops senses of touch and taste
Understands cold

Objective: The children will discover different forms of ice.

Materials:
- 13" by 9" by 2" cake pan
- Can opener
- Blender
- Ice crusher
- Cups
- Spoons
- Measuring cup
- One 6-ounce can of frozen grape juice concentrate
- Two trays of ice cubes

Procedure:

1. Put approximately 1" of water in the cake pan and place it outside if the temperature will be below 32° F during the night. If not, place the pan in a freezer overnight and discuss with the children how things freeze.

2. The next day, bring in the pan and let the children discover what has happened to the water. Explain briefly how water freezes when it reaches a certain temperature.

3. Show the trays of ice cubes. Then place them in an ice crusher, letting the children take turns crushing the ice.

4. Examine the ice pieces with the children. Are they smaller or larger than the ice cubes? Make five to six cups of finely crushed ice.

5. Now show the children the blender. Pour the juice concentrate into the chilled glass container of the electric blender.

6. Add the crushed ice, a cup at a time, into the blender. Blend well after each addition of ice.

7. Pour the grape icy mixture into small cups for the children to eat at once.

8. Discuss how we can eat the slushy grape frost, which is made of tiny pieces of ice. Point out the color of the icy mixture.

Variation/Way to Extend:

- Use orange, lemon, or fruit punch concentrate to also emphasize their respective colors. Can the children notice the different tastes?

I–95 WATER LENS

Subject Area: Science

Concepts/Skills: Explores surroundings
Develops powers of observation

Objective: The children will examine their room with a magnifying water lens.

Materials:
- Index cards
- Water
- Scissors
- Cellophane tape
- Plastic wrap

Procedure:

1. Explain that water can bend light in special ways. Prepare an index card for each child: cut out a hole in the center, about ½″ in diameter. Tape a piece of plastic wrap over the hole. Drop some water onto the plastic wrap. Let the children notice how the drop of water becomes rounded into the shape of a lens.

2. Hold the lens over something small, such as a picture in a book, and let the children see how it acts like a magnifier.

3. Let the children carefully examine objects around the room using their own individual lens.

Variation/Way to Extend:

- Read *Pete's Puddle* by Joanna Foster and Beatrice Darwin (San Diego: Harcourt Brace Jovanovich, Inc., 1969).

TRANSPORTATION

- ○ By Land
- ○ By Rail
- ○ By Water
- ○ By Air

   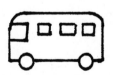

I-96   MOVING ON LAND

Subject Area: Language Arts

Concepts/Skills: Follows directions
Names pictured objects

Objective: The children will identify pictures of ways to travel on land.

Materials: • Display board
• Simple drawings of ways to travel on land

Procedure:

1. Ask children to tell some ways they can go from one place to another.
2. Introduce pictures and display asking the children to identify the way people are moving (traveling).
3. Ask them to point to the car, its wheels, its windows, and the place where the driver sits. Ask them to name the color and to count the wheels and windows.
4. Point to the horse. Name its body parts.
5. Explain that all the pictures show things that move people or objects from one place to another on land.

Variations/Ways to Extend:

• Put actual toy vehicles and animals in a box and have the children pick one out and find the picture that shows the same way of moving.
• Read the Caldecott Honor book *Truck* by Donald Crews (New York: Greenwillow, 1980).

I-97 PAPER CARS

Subject Area: Art

Concepts/Skills: Explores new materials
Coordinates use of eyes and hands
Applies glue and pastes things together

Objective: The children will construct cars from paper shapes.

Materials:
- Paper circles and rectangles
- Construction paper
- Glue
- Buttons
- Macaroni wheels

Procedure:

1. Discuss the idea of cars, trucks, and buses with the children. How do they come to school?
2. Give the children rectangles and circles to arrange and paste car shapes onto a sheet of paper.
3. Give them large buttons or macaroni wheels to glue on as car wheels.

Variations/Ways to Extend:

- Read *ABC of Cars and Trucks* by Anne Alexander (New York: Doubleday, 1971).
- Color small paper plates and paste a black circle in the center for a simpler activity making only a wheel. Insert a brad into the center of the plate and then into a small block of styrofoam to have a wheel that turns.
- Provide the children with lots of colored rectangles and circles and let them create make-believe things to ride in.

I–98   WHEELS ON THE BUS

Subject Area: Music

Concept/Skill: Listens to and repeats part of a song

Objectives: The children will learn a song about buses and add some lyrics of their own.

Material: • Words to the song (see Procedure section)

Procedure:

1. Teach the children this well-known nursery tune:

    The wheels on the bus go round and round,
    round and round, round and round.
    The wheels on the bus go round and round,
    as we ride to school.

2. Discuss what else happens on the bus and have the children make up new verses for the song. Some suggestions are: The windows on the bus go up and down; the horn on the bus goes beep, beep, beep; the windshield wipers go back and forth; the people on the bus go in and out.

Variation/Way to Extend:

• Read *Big Red Bus* by Ethel and Leonard Kessler (New York: Doubleday, 1964).

I-99   BIG TRUCK, LITTLE TRUCK

Subject Area: Math

Concepts/Skills: Groups things by size
Distinguises between "big" and "small"

Objectives: The children will identifty the small and big vehicles and place them in a small box or a big box accordingly.

Materials: • Large box
• Small box
• Table
• Large and small toy trucks, cars, vans, buses, and motorcycles

Procedure:

1. Place all the toys on a table.
2. Show the children a big toy and describe it as "big." Then show a small toy and describe it as "small."
3. Call on the children, one at a time, to find a big police car, a small fire truck, and so on.
4. Then ask the children to come to the table and select a toy and tell what it is, such as a big dump truck, for example.
5. Have the children then place the toys in the corresponding box. Small toys would go in the small box and large toys in the big box.

Variations/Ways to Extend:

• Sort the vehicles by color or category, such as all trucks or all cars.
• Read *Red Light Green Light* by Golden MacDonald (New York: Doubleday, 1944).

I-100   PRETZEL WHEELS

Subject Area: Nutrition/Foods Experience

Concepts/Skills: Identifies circle
Develops fine motor movements of rolling, shaping, and pounding

Objectives: The children will mix and form pretzel wheels.

Materials:
- Pictures or models of wheels
- Recipe and ingredients for pretzels
- Large bowl
- Spatula
- Measuring spoons
- Measuring cup
- Greased cookie sheet

- Cooling rack
- Floured board
- Beater
- Oven
- Brush
- Kosher salt

Procedure:

1. Follow this recipe to make pretzel wheels:

   1 package yeast
   1 teaspoon sugar
   1 teaspoon salt
   1½ cups warm water
   4 cups flour
   1 egg, separated

   Dissolve yeast in warm water. Then add the other ingredients (except the egg) and mix until the dough forms a ball. Knead until smooth on a floured surface. Pull off a ball the size of a walnut. Roll like a snake and then shape it into a circle. Roll out other small straight pieces to make spokes. Separate an egg and beat the egg white. Place the wheels on the greased cookie sheet. Brush with egg white and sprinkle with kosher salt. Bake at 425° F for 12 to 15 minutes and then let cool on a rack.

2. Enjoy the pretzel wheels for a snack.

Variations/Ways to Extend:

- Show several pictures of wheels and discuss their shape and uses. Be sure to gear this to the children's interest in wagons, toys, shopping carts, and so on.)
- Display the ingredients and utensils for the pretzel wheels and have the children identify each one.
- Listen to the "Car Song" on *Songs to Grow On,* Volume 1, by Woody Guthrie, available from Folkways Records, 43 West 61st Street, New York, New York 10023.

I–101   BLOCK TRAIN

Subject Area: Thinking Games

Concepts/Skills: Shows simple symbolic play
Names pictured objects
Cooperates in a group

Objective: The children will construct trains from their unit blocks.

Materials: • Unit blocks
• Other block sets
• Pictures of trains

Procedure:

1. Make use of the block corner for this activity. Talk to the children about trains and show pictures of trains from books or room display.
2. Divide the class into small groups and give each group a pile of blocks. Vary the sizes, shapes, and colors of the blocks to add interest.
3. Encourage each group to make a train from the blocks. They may wish to make a long, straight train or a circular one going around them.
4. Add appropriate props for dramatic play.

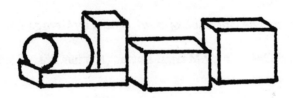

Variation/Way to Extend:

• Have each child choose a block to work with. Assist each child in tracing around the block with a large marker or large crayon. Do this several times on a sheet of white paper for their own "trains" to take home.

Weekly Subtheme: By Rail

I-102 TRAIN CUTOUTS

Subject Area: Social Studies

Concepts/Skills: Shows curiosity and interest in surroundings
Applies glue

Objectives: The children will identify train pictures and mount them.

Materials:
- Magazines or coloring books with train pictures
- Colored oaktag cut into small rectangles
- Scissors
- Paste

Procedure:

1. With the children, look through magazines and/or coloring books for pictures of or about trains and train personnel. Try to find large, clear pictures of engines and cabooses.
2. Cut the pictures out and have each child select the one he or she likes best.
3. Help the children mount each picture onto a colored oaktag rectangle.
4. Make a wall display of the pictures in the classroom and invite each child to make up a sentence about what is happening in the picture.

Variations/Ways to Extend:

- Look at the pictures in *The Big Book of Real Trains* by George Zaffo (New York: Grosset & Dunlap, 1970).
- Read *The Little Red Caboose* by Marian Potter (Racine Wis.: Golden Press, 1953).

I-103 MY SHAPE TRAIN

Subject Area: Art

Concepts/Skills: Follows directions
Develops fine motor actions of cutting and pasting

Objective: The children will make an engine and box cars by pasting shapes.

Materials: • Colored construction paper to cut into train shapes
• One 12″ by 18″ piece of white paper for each child
• Black markers
• Paste
• Scissors

Procedure:

1. Distribute the white paper
2. Give the children the precut rectangles and circles.
3. Assist them in laying the shapes out in a train pattern on their papers.
4. Paste in place.

Variations/Ways to Extend:

• Read the Caldecott Honor book *Freight Train* by Donald Crews (New York: Greenwillow, 1978).
• Sing the American folk song "Down by the Station" with the children. Words can be found in the songbook *Eye Winker, Tom Tinker, Chin Chopper* by Tom Glazer (Garden City, New York: Doubleday, 1972).

I–104 BOX TRAIN RIDE

Subject Area: Creative Dramatics/Movement

Concepts/Skills: Identifies colors
Follows directions
Participates in singing

Objectives: The children will identify the colors of the train box cars, sing, and pretend they are riding a train.

Materials:
- Three large corrugated boxes large enough for a two-year-old to sit in
- Cellophane tape
- Engineer or conductor's hat
- Red scarf
- Record of train sound effects
- 12" by 18" sheets of red, blue, and yellow paper
- Words to song (see Procedure section)

Procedure:

1. Place the boxes on the floor in a row to form a train.
2. Tape the colored paper on each box side that faces the children, making one car red, one blue, and one yellow.
3. Select several children at a time to be passengers and ride the train.
4. Select one to be engineer and let that child wear the hat and scarf. Direct the engineer to sit in a particular color car.
5. Ask the other children to name who is sitting in a particular car and vice versa. "Who is sitting in the red car?" "Which color car is Judy sitting in?"
6. Tell the children to pretend to go for a ride. Tell the engineer to call out "All Aboard."
7. Accompany the children's play with recorded train noises from a sound effects record and have all the passengers and other children sing the following to the tune of "Row, Row, Row Your Boat":

   Ride, ride, ride the train,
   Quickly down the track.
   Clickety, clickety, clickety clack,
   When will you be back?

8. Have the children move their arms back and forth like the wheel motion of the train.
9. Empty the train and repeat the process with the other children.
10. Ask the children not on the train to pretend they are on the platform at the station waving "hello" or "goodbye."

Variations/Ways to Extend:

- Number the cars in sequence for number recognition with older children.
- Give directions of positional concepts with the cars, such as between the red and yellow cars or in the blue car.
- Have the letters on the cars correspond to initial letters of the children's names. "Which car has the first letter of your name, Sam?"

I-105 ALL ABOARD FOR BREAKFAST

Subject Area: Nutrition/Foods Experience

Concepts/Skills: Knows that different activities go on at different times of the day
Follows simple directions

Objectives: The children will make French toast and form a dining car from the toast and sausage.

Materials:
- Enriched or wheat bread, sliced
- Butter
- Eggs (enough for class)
- 2 tablespoons milk per egg
- Package of breakfast sausage (organic if available)
- Griddles
- Whip for mixing

- Pancake turner
- Vanilla
- Syrup
- Plates
- Silverware
- Napkins
- Bowl

Procedure:

1. Explain how people take trains for long trips and must eat and sleep on the train.
2. Show the ingredients and utensils. Discuss what could be made from the ingredients. Discuss what was eaten for breakfast by the children.
3. Demonstrate how French toast is made. Divide the class into groups of four (or more if practical) and help the children dip and fry the French toast. (**Caution:** Be sure the children do not touch the hot griddles.) Fry the sausage in a separate pan, turning often.
4. Cut the toast in half. Cut the sausage into wheel disks. Place the wheels on the bottom of the half slice of French toast to form a dining car.
5. Add syrup, cut, and eat.

Variations/Ways to Extend:

- Have the children sit in chairs arranged like a train while they wait their turn for a plate.
- Go on pretend trips with the train. Encourage the children to say what they see out the train windows.

I-106   SAIL AWAY SAILBOAT

Subject Areas: Art and Science

Concepts/Skills: Develops fine motor movement of assembling parts
Follows directions
Observes floating

Objectives: The children will assemble a sailboat and float it on water.

Materials: • Styrofoam meat trays cut in boat shape
• White paper triangles
• Round wooden toothpicks (use lollypop sticks for larger boats)
• Pictures of sailboats
• White glue
• Pan of water

Procedure:

1. Distribute the boat shapes. Ask the children what they could make from the shape. Indicate appreciation for the children's various ideas.
2. Show the pictures of the sailboats. Explain how the purpose of the sail is to catch the wind so it can push the boat across the water.
3. Give the children the triangle sails and discuss the shape. Distribute the tooth picks.
4. Put glue on three-fourths of the toothpick and glue the sail to it. Press the remaining one-fourth of the toothpick into the styrofoam near its center.
5. Demonstrate how the boat can be sailed in a pan of water by blowing on the sail.
6. Let the children sail their sailboats in the water.

Variations/Ways to Extend:

• Make the sails in various colors for color identification.
• Put each child's first initial on a different sail for letter identification.

I–107   TUNA BOATS

Subject Areas: Nutrition/Foods Experience and Social Studies

Concepts/Skills: Develops fine motor movement of mixing
Develops senses of touch, smell, and taste

Objectives: The children will make and eat a tuna boat.

Materials:
- Canned tuna fish, drained
- Can opener
- Celery, washed
- Mayonnaise
- Hot dog rolls
- Bowl
- Fork
- Knife
- Spoon
- Paper plates
- Napkins
- Pictures of tuna boats
  (a good source is *National Geographic* magazine)

Procedure:

1. Explain that most of the fish we eat is caught on fishing boats. Explain that tuna is a large ocean fish caught from large fishing boats. Display the pictures of tuna boats.
2. Ask the students if their parents buy tuna fish. What does it come in?
3. Show the can(s) of tuna fish for today's activity. Explain to the children that today they are going to make tuna boats to eat, not to sail. Show the other utensils and ingredients they'll be using. Have the children identify each one.
4. Place the drained tuna in a bowl and mash with a fork.
5. Show the celery before and after dicing and then add it to the tuna. Add enough mayonnaise to moisten and mix well.
6. Distribute the hot dog rolls. Ask the children to open the rolls and spoon tuna fish onto each one. (You may want to cut each "boat" in half for easier handling by the children.)
7. Let the children pretend the rolls and tuna are boats to sail into their mouths. (Be sure the children take small bites.)

Variations/Ways to Extend:

- Make a sail from a straw and a piece of paper and stand it in the tuna boat before the children start eating. Be sure they remove the sail before taking any bites.
- Teach the children "Row, Row, Row Your Boat."

I-108 ALUMINUM BOAT

Subject Area: Science

Concepts/Skills: Makes observations
Tests floating ability of different containers

Objective: The children will observe how the shape of an object helps it float.

Materials:
- Aluminum foil, square pieces
- Large bowl of water
- Pictures of large and small ships

Procedure:

1. Explain that sometimes we wonder how something as big and heavy as a boat can float. Display pictures of ships. The boat or ship must be made to hold a lot of air, which is lighter than water.
2. Show the pieces of aluminum foil. Help the children form the little row boats by turning up the edges.
3. Place them carefully on top of the water in the bowl. Let several children experiment with the foil.

Variations/Ways to Extend:

- Add pennies or other small weights to the boats and see them sink further into the water. Experiment with sinking and floating.
- Read *Mr. Grumpy's Outing* by John Burningham (New York: Holt, Rinehart & Winston, 1971).
- Experiment with various sizes and shapes of containers and boxes, such as an empty round salt box, small wooden matchboxes, plastic margarine tub, and a cigar box. Let the children guess whether a container will float or not before actually trying it out.

I-109 SAND BOAT PICTURE

Subject Area: Art

Concepts/Skills: Develops fine motor movements of filling, dumping, and tracing
Expresses creatively
Learns about boat shapes

Objective: The children will create boat pictures by squeezing out a design with sand.

Materials:
- Large drawing paper
- Squeeze-bottle glue
- Pencils
- Sand
- Powdered paint
- Containers or margarine tubs
- One boat pattern for each child

Procedure:

1. Mix the powdered paint with fine sand to the desired shade.
2. Let each child place a tugboat pattern on a sheet of drawing paper. Help the child to trace around the boat.
3. Help the child squeeze out the glue around the boat shape. Let the child complete the remainder of the design by squeezing glue within the boat shape in whatever design wanted.
4. Have each child fill a container with some of the colored sand and then dump it all over the picture.
5. Ask the children to shake off the excess sand and allow the glue to dry. Explain that the sand will adhere to the glue for a lovely design inside the boat shape.

Variation/Way to Extend:

- Read *Boat Book* by Gail Gibbons (New York: Holiday House, 1983).

I-110   SAILBOAT SONG

Subject Area: Music

Concepts/Skills: Develops sense of rhythm
Listens to and follows directions

Objective: The children will learn a song about boats.

Material: • Words to the song (see Procedure section)

Procedure:

1. Sing the following song to the tune of "Frère Jacques":

   Boats are sailing, boats are sailing,
   In the sea, in the sea.
   Floating all around us, floating all around us,
   Look and see, look and see.

2. Encourage the children to move around the room as you sing, pretending they are boats sailing on the water.
3. At the end of the song show the children how to pretend to look out in the sea and see boats.

Variations/Ways to Extend:

   • Sing the song while the children engage in water play.
   • Give the children small toy boats to float in a large plastic tub of water.

I-111   PINWHEEL PROPELLER

Subject Area: Science

Concepts/Skills: Makes observations
Tests effect of wind
Uses adults as resources for help

Objectives: The children will construct pinwheels and observe how air makes things move.

Materials: • Construction paper cut in squares
• Scissors
• Pins
• Pencils

Procedure:

1. Talk about propellers, the parts of some airplanes and helicopters that help make them fly. Tell the children they will pretend their little pinwheels are propellers.
2. Help each child cut construction paper on a diagonal from each corner of the square. Stop before reaching the center.

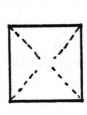 

3. As you face each triangular section, fold the upper right-hand corner down toward the center. Insert a pin through the center and attach the paper to the eraser end of a pencil. Show the children how it turns.
4. Invite the children to blow on their propellers or wave pieces of cardboard in front of them. Explain how air makes things move.

Variation/Way to Extend:

• Look at the pictures in *The First Book of Airplanes* by Jeanne Bendick (New York: Watts, 1982).

I-112 AIRPLANE SNACK

Subject Area: Nutrition/Foods Experience

Concepts/Skills: Develops fine motor movements of rolling and shaping
Develops senses of smell, taste, and touch

Objective: The children will make edible airplanes for snack.

Materials:
- ½ cup corn syrup
- ½ cup peanut butter
- 3 cups toasted rice cereal
- Pictures of airplanes
- Bowl
- Spoon
- Wax paper
- Teaspoon

Procedure:

1. Talk about the shape of an airplane and show several pictures.
2. In a bowl, combine the corn syrup and peanut butter. Then stir in the cereal.
3. Drop batter from a teaspoon onto wax paper.
4. Help each child mold two log shapes and crisscross them to form an airplane. These edible airplanes can either be stored or eaten immediately.

Variation/Way to Extend:

- Discuss how airplane personnel often serve food to passengers while flying.

I-113   FLY OR STOP?

Subject Area: Gross Motor Games

Concepts/Skills: Develops listening abilities
Develops body coordination

Objectives: The children will pretend to be airplanes and listen for signals to fly or stop.

Materials: • Record player
• Record of instrumental music
• Large open area

Procedure:

1. Tell the children to pretend to be airplanes flying around the room (spread arms and move smoothly around area). Play some instrumental music to accompany their flying.
2. Every time you stop the music, they must stop flying. Start the music, and they fly away again.
3. Suggestion: Choose an instrumental piece from Hap Palmer's album, *Movin'*, available from Educational Activities, Inc., Freeport, N. Y. 11520.

Variation/Way to Extend:

• Watch a film together about planes, such as trick flyers or crop dusters, and then have the children pretend to be piloting one of these planes.

I–114   TWINKLE, TWINKLE, LITTLE STAR

Subject Area: Music

Concepts/Skills: Develops gross motor movement of walking on tiptoe
Develops listening ability
Sings parts of a song

Objectives: The children will listen to a song about a star and sing it.

Material: • Words to the song "Twinkle, Twinkle, Little Star"

Procedure:

1. Have the children listen to you sing the words to this well-known nursery tune.
2. Talk about how stars are out in space, far above airplanes flying.
3. Repeat the song, teaching the children to act out these movements:

> Twinkle, twinkle, little star (*walk on tiptoe*)
> How I wonder what you are (*stretch hands overhead*).
> Up above the world so high (*sway back and forth*)
> Like a diamond in the sky (*sway back and forth*).
> Twinkle, twinkle, little star (*walk on tiptoe*)
> How I wonder what you are (*stretch hands overhead*).

Variation/Way to Extend:

• Make a large paper star for each child and let each child glue glitter onto the star. Attach two long pieces of yarn to the star and tie around the child's neck for him or her to wear while acting out the song.

I–115   WOODEN GLIDER PICTURES

Subject Area: Art

Concepts/Skills: Develops fine motor movements of applying glue and pasting
Follows directions
Paints with a large brush

Objective: The children will make simple gliders from tongue depressors.

Materials:
- Two tongue depressors per child
- White chalk
- White glue
- Blue construction paper
- Cotton balls
- Primary colored paint
- Paintbrushes
- Smocks
- Toy glider

Procedure:

1. Show the toy glider and explain how it floats through the air without a motor.
2. Give each child two tongue depressors. Explain that these are made of wood.
3. Let the children select a color to paint their sticks.
4. When the paint is dry, help the children glue their two sticks together, one on top of the other, to make a flat glider.
5. Then help the children glue their gliders onto blue paper.
6. Draw outlines of white clouds on the blue paper with chalk and have the children glue cotton balls inside the outlines to complete the glider pictures.

Variations/Ways to Extend:

- Make a large class mural with gliders flying amid cotton clouds.
- Fly a wooden toy glider in a large area or outdoors. Let the children take turns flying the glider while the other children sit a safe distance away. (If two adults are supervising the group, have two toy gliders available. This will allow the children to have the fun of trying out the gliders in half the time.)

ANIMALS

○ Forest Animals

○ Pets

○ Zoo Animals

○ The Circus and Circus Animals

I-116   TWO LITTLE BLACKBIRDS

Subject Area: Language Arts

Concepts/Skills: Imitates actions
Follows directions
Repeats parts of a fingerplay

Objective: The children will demonstrate the action of a fingerplay.

Materials: • Words to the fingerplay (see Procedure section)
• Cellophane tape
• Two strips of black construction paper ¾″ wide for each child
• Two 2″ by ½″ pieces of black construction paper for each child

Procedure:

1. Tape one ¾″-wide strip onto each child's index finger.
2. Take the 2″ by ½″ strips and tape them so that they are at a right angle to the finger band. Bend upward to form black "wings."
3. Fit these wings over the children's right and left index fingers.

4. While they are wearing these little "blackbirds," teach the children the following fingerplay to dramatize:

> Two little blackbirds sitting on a hill (*place an index finger on each shoulder*),
> One named Jack (*hold one finger out*),
> One named Jill (*hold other finger out*).
> Fly away, Jack. Fly away, Jill (*make one finger, then the other, fly away*).
> Come back, Jack. Come back, Jill (*bring fingers to perch on shoulders again one at a time*).

Variations/Ways to Extend:

• Make a copy of the fingerplay for each child and tape the blackbird finger bands onto the paper for the children to use at home.
• Read the Caldecott Honor book *Play with Me* by Marie H. Ets (New York: Viking, 1955).

Weekly Subtheme: Forest Animals

I-117 COTTON RABBIT

Subject Area: Art

Concepts/Skills: Develops fine motor movements of pasting and tearing paper
Learns about rabbits
Looks at books

Objective: The children will construct pictures of bunnies.

Materials:
- Bunny patterns (see next page)
- Cotton
- Paper
- Ribbon or bows
- Pipe cleaners
- Glue
- Scissors
- Crayons
- Picture books about bunnies

Procedure:
1. Give each child a copy of one of the bunny patterns.
2. Let the children cover the rabbit's body with paste and then cover the glued area with cotton. Use cotton for the tail and feet too.
3. Give the children some paper and show them how to tear two long strips for bunny ears. Then ask each child to tear two ears and paste them on top of the bunnies' heads.
4. Have the children glue a bow or ribbon around the rabbit's neck and use different lengths of thin pipe cleaners to paste on as whiskers.
5. Let each child draw the mouth and eyes on his or her bunny.
6. Encourage the children to look at picture books of rabbits to further their understanding of this animal.

Variations/Ways to Extend:
- Read *Pat the Bunny* by Dorothy Kunhardt (Racine, Wis.: Western, 1942).
- Listen to a recording of "Bunny Hop" and have the children jump along to the music.

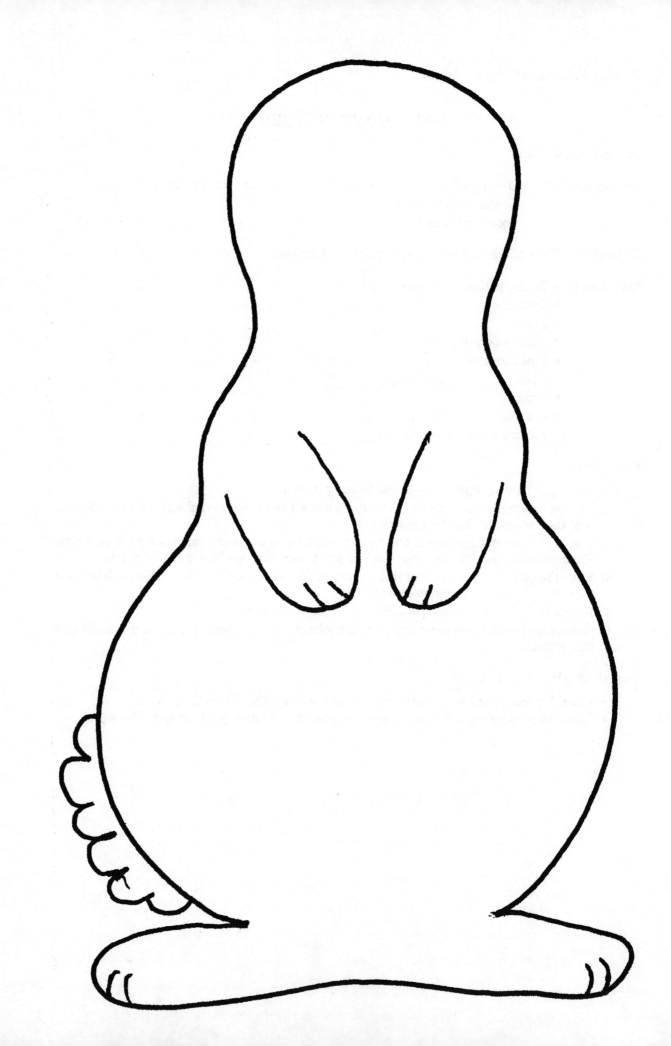

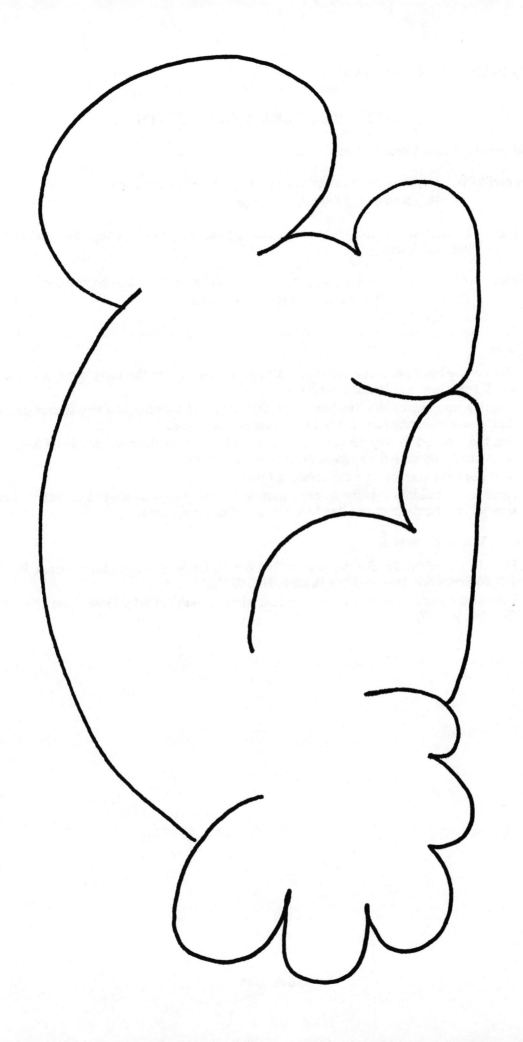

Weekly Subtheme: Forest Animals

I–118 TURTLES AND RABBITS

Subject Area: Gross Motor Games

Concepts/Skills: Develops gross motor movements of jumping and crawling
Points to body parts when named

Objectives: The children will move across the room, jump with two feet together, and crawl on hands and knees.

Materials:
- Masking tape marking off a starting line and a finishing line on the floor
- Pictures of turtles and rabbits (or stuffed toys)
- Smocks

Procedure:

1. Review the body parts of a turtle and a rabbit. Then review the body parts of children—head, arms, legs, hands, knees, and feet.
2. Wearing smocks, the children jump with their two feet together and two fingers on top of their heads as bunny ears. Let them hop around the room.
3. Ask the children to stop jumping and to scrunch down on their forearms and knees, pull their smocks up onto their heads, and crawl like turtles.
4. Now show the starting line and finishing line.
5. Arrange the children in pairs. Ask one partner to jump like a rabbit and the other to crawl slowly like a turtle from one line to the other. Who finishes first?

Variations/Ways to Extend:

- Play the record "Walk Like the Animals" by Kimbo Records (Kimbo Educational, P.O. Box 477, 86 South 5th Avenue, Long Branch, N.J. 07723).
- Look at the pictures in the Caldecott medal winner *Noah's Ark* by Peter Spier (New York, Doubleday, 1977).

I–119 BEAD SNAKE

Subject Area: Math

Concepts/Skills Develops fine motor movement of stringing five large beads
Matches colors
Counts to two or more

Objectives: The children will string five beads of the same color to make a snake.

Materials: • Five large matching beads for each child
• String or cord for each child

Procedure:

1. Name the colors of the beads distributed. With each child, count out five beads of the same color.
2. Demonstrate how to string them. Tell the children to string all five beads to make a snake shape.
3. When they have finished stringing the beads, have them pull this string across a table, moving from side to side like a snake.
4. Ask the children to make the *s* sound as they move their snakes. Tell them, "*S* is a letter that says 's-s-s-s,' just like a snake!"

Variations/Ways to Extend:

• Call out or hold up a particular color bead and see if the children can match it to their bead snake of the same color. Ask the children to either hold up their snake or move it along when they hear or see their color.
• Read *My Very First Book of Numbers* by Eric Carle (New York: Harper & Row, Pub., 1974).

I-120   TEDDY BEAR

Subject Area: Music

Concepts/Skills: Follows directions
Develops body coordination

Objective: The children will act out a song about teddy bears.

Material: • Words to the song (see Procedure section)

Procedure:

1.   Repeat the following song twice for the children:

> Teddy bear, teddy bear, turn around,
> Teddy bear, teddy bear, touch the ground
> Teddy bear, teddy bear, shine your shoes,
> Teddy bear, teddy bear, that will do.
> Teddy bear, teddy bear, climb the stairs,
> Teddy bear, teddy bear, say your prayers.
> Teddy bear, teddy bear, shut the light,
> Teddy bear, teddy bear, say "good night."

2.   Have the children imitate your actions as they learn to act out each line of the song.

Variations/Ways to Extend:

• Read *I Am a Mouse* (Racine, Wis.: Western, 1970) and *I Am a Bear* (Racine, Wis.: Western, 1970), both by Ole Risom.
• Give each child a copy of the teddy bear pattern and have the children glue fake fur scraps onto their shape. Also cut out eyes, noses, and mouths for the children to glue onto the bear.

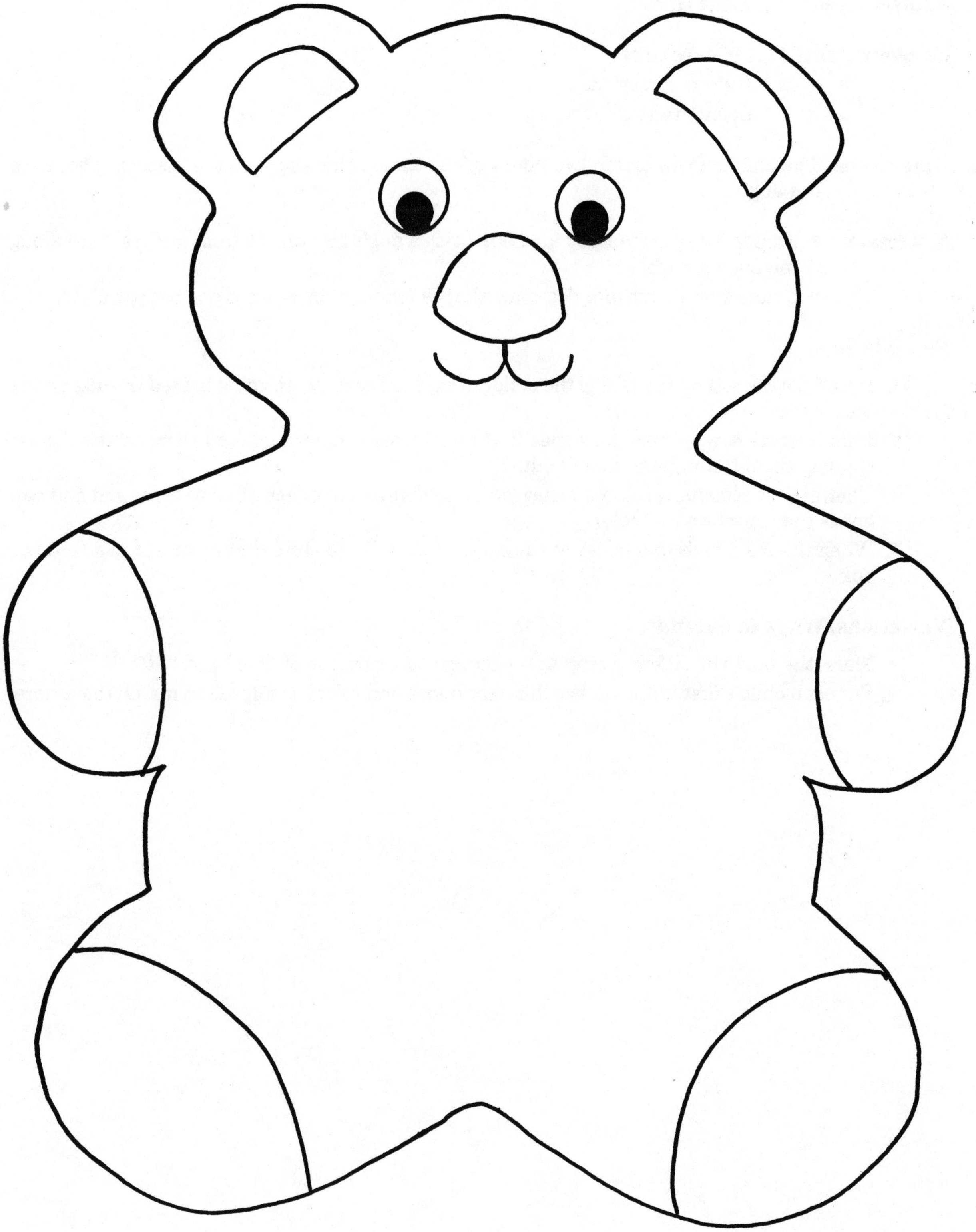

Weekly Subtheme: Pets

I-121 MATCH THE BONE

Subject Area: Thinking Games

Concepts/Skills: Matches colors
Follows directions
Counts to two

Objectives: The children will match two bones of the same color and feed the matching bones to the dog.

Materials:
- Empty dog biscuit or dog food box (with a dog's face on the front and a slit cut along the dog's mouth)
- Colored paper cut into dog bone shapes (enough for at least one set per child)

Procedure:

1. Introduce the activity by telling the children that today they are going to feed the dog on the box.
2. Demonstrate how to find two bones that are the same color and feed them to the dog by slipping them through the mouth slit.
3. Then set the remaining colored bones out on a table and ask each child to come and find two bones that are the same color.
4. When the child finds two bones of the same color, tell the child that he or she can feed the dog.

Variations/Ways to Extend:

- Make the bones of different sizes to encourage comparisons of "big" and "little."
- Put each child's first initial on two different bones and ask the children to match the letters.

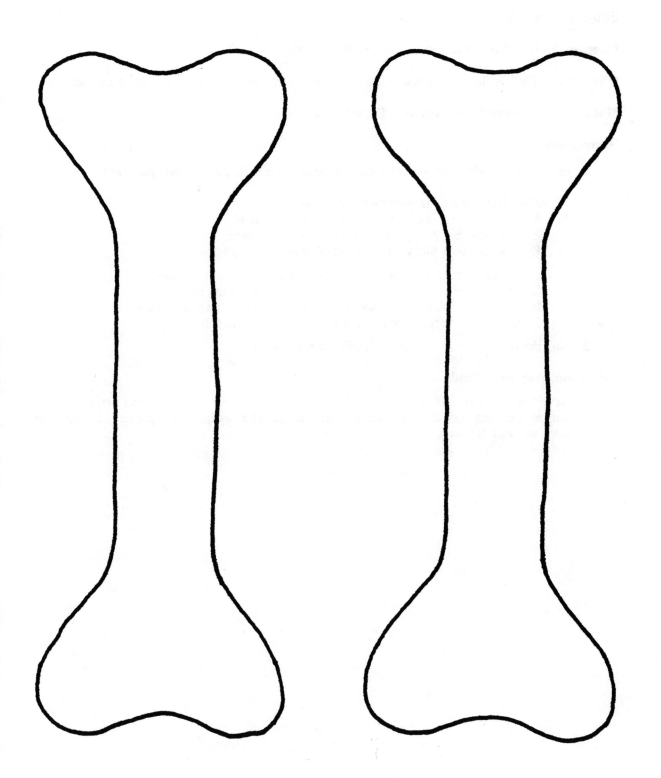

I-122   MARY HAD A LITTLE LAMB

Subject Area: Music

Concept/Skill: Participates in and responds to music

Objective: The children will become familiar with a popular nursery song about a pet lamb.

Material: • Words to the song (see Procedure section)

Procedure:

1. Introduce this 100-year-old traditional song about a little girl and her pet lamb.

   Mary had a little lamb, little lamb, little lamb;
   Mary had a little lamb, its fleece was white as snow.
   Everywhere that Mary went, Mary went, Mary went;
   Everywhere that Mary went, the lamb was sure to go.

   It followed her to school one day, school one day, school one day;
   It followed her to school one day, which was against the rule.
   It made the children laugh and play, laugh and play, laugh and play;
   It made the children laugh and play, to see a lamb in school.

2. Sing the song often so the children will learn the words.

Variation/Way to Extend:

• Have the children take turns being "Mary" or "Marty" (for the boys) and acting out the song as it is sung. Tell the children that they may hold a toy lamb or a picture of a lamb, or act it out with a friend.

Weekly Subtheme: Pets

I–123 CAT ON THE FENCE

Subject Area: Language Arts

Concepts/Skills: Imitates actions of adults
Acts out a simple story
Develops gross motor movements of hopping, walking, and jumping

Objectives: The children will participate in an action poem about a pet cat.

Material: • Words to the fingerplay (see Procedure section)

Procedure:

1. Introduce the children to the following fingerplay:

    When everyone is fast asleep (*clasp hands, put up to cheek and tilt head*),
    My cat goes out to play.
    He leaps up on the tall, high fence (*jump in place on two feet*)
    And walks along the way (*Walking motion with feet*).
    First one foot and then the other (*lift one foot high, then the other foot*)
    Slowly walking, slowly stalking;
    That big white cat of mine (*sway body from side to side slowly*).

2. Repeat the fingerplay several times with the children.

Variations/Ways to Extend:

*   Place a long strip of string, yarn, or tape on the floor. Have the children practice walking on it, pretending they are on a "tall, high fence."
*   Use this fingerplay as a stimulus for an easel painting subject.

Weekly Subtheme: Pets

I-124 FINGER-PAINTED PET

Subject Area: Art

Concepts/Skills: Develops fine motor movements of finger dexterity and strength
Makes a choice
Explores different mediums
Expresses creatively

Objective: The children will create finger paintings of favorite pets.

Materials: • Finger paints
• Large pet animal shapes cut from glazed paper or newsprint

Procedure:

1. Cut out shapes of dogs, cats, birds, hamsters, fish, and turtles. (The patterns shown here will help get you started.)
2. Let the children select the shape(s) they want to use.
3. With commercial finger paints or finger paints made from the recipe given below, have the children finger-paint directly onto the shapes. (Recipe: Add liquid laundry starch to powdered tempera paints and whip to a consistency of heavy cream.)

Variations/Ways to Extend:

• Read *One Little Kitten* by Tana Hoban (New York: Greenwillow, 1979).
• Play the song "Doggie in the Window" by Golden Records (AA Records, 250 West 57th Street, New York, N.Y. 10019).
• Read the poem "Aquarium" by Valerie Worth, found in her book *Small Poems* (New York: Farrar, Straus & Giroux, 1972).

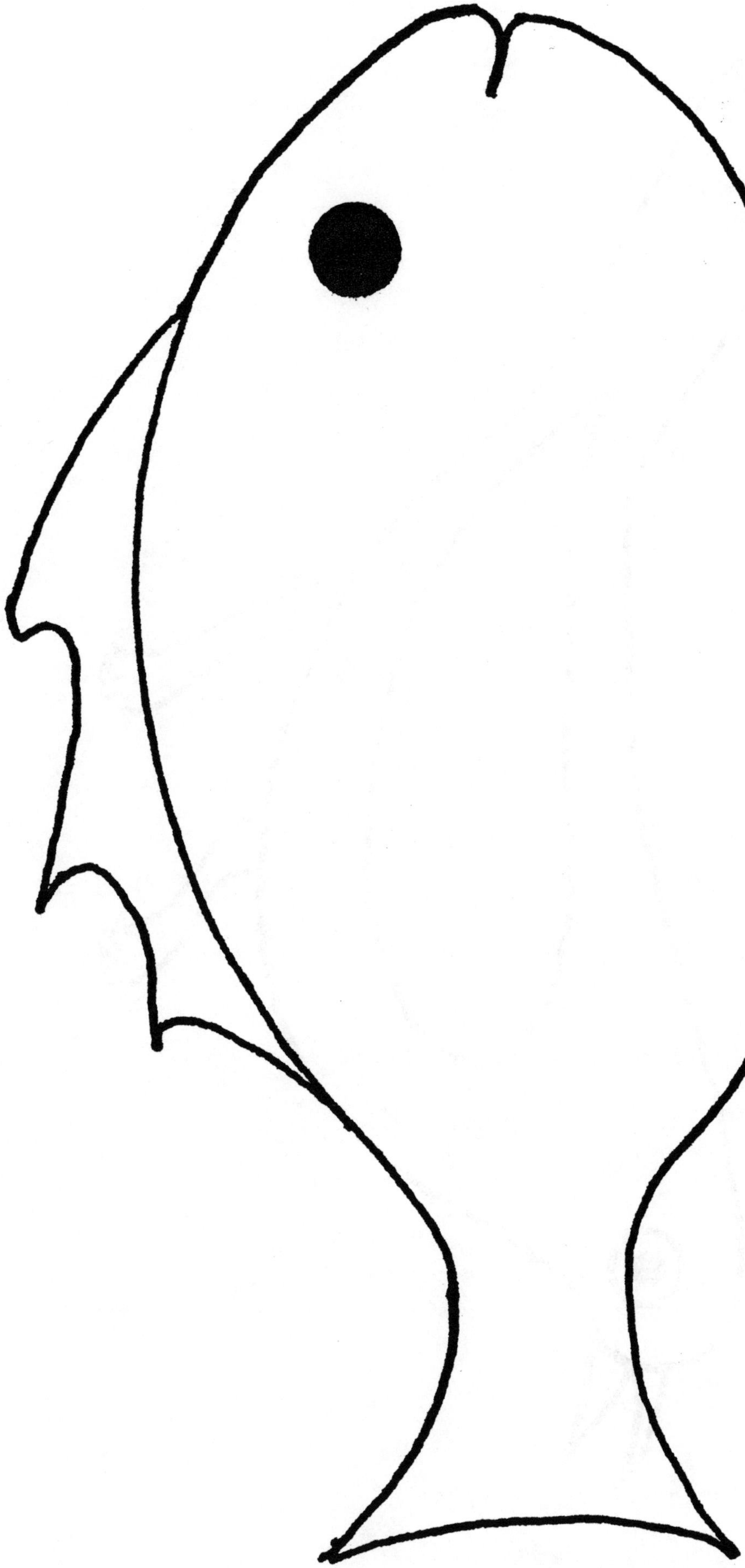

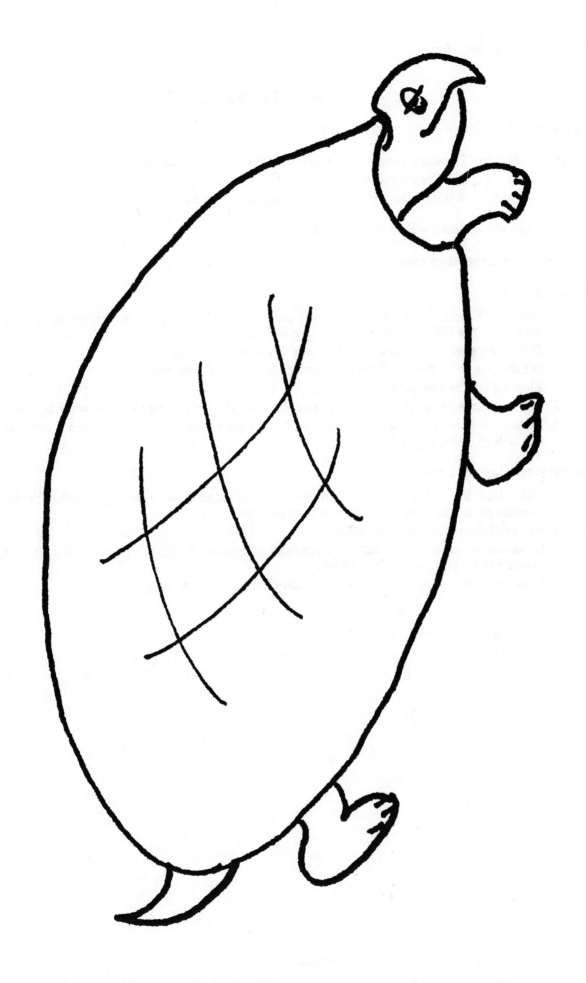

Weekly Subtheme: Pets

I-125   THE WAYS PETS MOVE

Subject Area: Creative Dramatics/Movement

Concepts/Skills: Develops gross motor movement of body coordination
Follows directions
Knows difference between walking and running

Objectives: The children will move to directions given.

Material: • Large open area

Procedure:

1. Give the children the opportunity to walk and run while listening to instructions. Make sure they know the difference between walking and running.
2. Divide the group into pairs. One child is a dog; the other, a cat.
3. Let the dog chase the cat. When caught, the cat becomes the dog.
4. Then let one be a cat; the other, a bird.
5. Play the same game, with the cat chasing the bird who is flapping its wings while running.
6. Then let the children slowly walk in a circle like guinea pigs or move their arms to swim as fish or leap about like frogs.

Variations/Ways to Extend:

• Make flour dough available and let the children use animal cookie cutters to make shapes. Encourage the children to create their own pet shapes, too.
• Eat goldfish crackers at snack time.
• Order the five-piece puzzle "Kitten" from Judy Instructional Aids (The Judy Company, 250 James Street, Morristown, N.J. 07960).
• Read *Who Said Meow?* by Maria Polushkin (New York: Crown, 1975).

I-126   WHAT'S IN THE CAGE?

Subject Area: Social Studies

Concept/Skill: Puts together two or more words to form a simple sentence

Objectives: The children will develop curiosity and interest in zoo animals and identify some of them.

Materials:
- Coloring book
- Scissors
- Shoe box
- Glue
- Oaktag or cardboard
- Clear, self-stick vinyl
- Permanent marker

Procedure:

1. Prepare the pictures ahead of time. Cut out and color the coloring book pictures and mount each one on cardboard or oaktag.
2. Cover a shoe box with clear, self-stick vinyl and draw black stripes on it to create a cage.
3. Put the pictures of the tigers, lions, leopards, monkeys, bears, birds, reptiles, fish, elephants, giraffes, and other zoo animals into the box.
4. Ask each child to pick an animal, name it, and tell something about it.
5. Display each picture after it has been discussed.

Variations/Ways to Extend:

- Make individual cages by pasting pictures onto matchboxes for the children to take home.
- If possible, find a big picture book of zoo animals with good, realistic, color pictures. Cut out, mount, and laminate these pictures for use year after year.

I–127   ELEPHANT WALK

Subject Areas: Music and Creative Dramatics/Movement

Concepts/Skills: Follows directions
Develops gross motor skill of body coordination

Objectives: The children will participate in a song about the zoo and move accordingly.

Materials: • Words to the song (see Procedure section)
• Pictures of zoo animals
• Large open area
• Records about the zoo

Procedure:
1. Show pictures of zoo animals and listen to some records about the zoo, such as "Going to the Zoo" on *Folk Song Carnival* by Hap Palmer (Educational Activities, Inc., Box 392, Freeport, N.Y. 11520).
2. Demonstrate some animal walks and have the children join in. For example, you might show an elephant walk by bending over at the waist, extending your arms, and joining your hands in a clasp. Then walk around the room slowly, swinging your "trunk."
3. Sing the following song while animal walking:

> This is the way an elephant walks, an elephant walks, an elephant walks
> This is the way an elephant walks, at the zoo.

4. Continue singing and acting out other animal walks, such as "a monkey climbs," "a lion stalks," and "a seal swims."

Variation/Way to Extend:

• Read the award-winning book *One, Two, Three to the Zoo* by Eric Carle (Cleveland, Ohio: Collins Publishers, 1968).

I–128 STUFFED ANIMAL DAY

Subject Area: Language Arts

Concepts/Skills: Places objects in, on, beside, under, and behind
Follows directions

Objective: The children will respond to prepositions that instruct them in what to do with stuffed animals.

Materials:
- Assortment of stuffed animals (could be brought in by children)
- Animal stickers
- Table and chair

Procedure:

1. Use the school's stuffed animal toys or send a letter home in advance asking parents to allow children to bring in their favorite stuffed animal toys. Be sure each is labeled with the child's name.
2. Display all the teddy bears, elephants, seals, penguins, horses, lambs, and other creatures you may have collected.
3. When ready, have each child pick up their own animal or their choice of school animals. Identify types of animals and let the children talk about them.
4. Instruct the children individually to put their animal in the chair, on the table, beside the chair, under the chair, under the table, and behind the chair. Try other variations and add more prepositions to make the activity more difficult. You might also give some humorous directions, too.
5. Reward each child for his or her effort with an animal sticker.

Variations/Ways to Extend:
- Serve animal-shaped cookies at snack time.
- Let the children play "zoo" with all the stuffed animals.

I-129   ANIMAL BREAD TREATS

Subject Area: Nutrition/Foods Experience

Concepts/Skills: Develops fine motor movements of rolling, cutting and spreading
Knows the names of at least three animals

Objective: The children will create zoo animal bread treats.

Materials:
- Whole-wheat bread slices
- Rolling pin
- Plastic knives
- Softened butter or margarine
- Animal cookie cutters
- Small cut-up pieces of cheese
- Juice

Procedure:

1. Show the animal cookie cutters and help the children identify each animal.
2. Demonstrate how to flatten the bread with a rolling pin.
3. Have the children flatten bread slices and then press down and cut the bread with the animal cookie cutters.
4. Spread each animal shape with butter or margarine and decorate with cut-up bits of cheese as facial features.
5. Enjoy these animal bread treats with juice at snack time.

Variation/Way to Extend:

- Read *Everybody Has a House and Everybody Eats* by Mary M. Green (Reading, Mass.: Addison-Wesley, 1961).

I–130 LION FACES

Subject Area: Art

Concepts/Skills: Becomes familiar with the shape "circle" and the color "yellow"
Develops fine motor movements of painting and pasting
Knows facial features

Objectives: The children will construct and paint a lion's face.

Materials:
- Large white paper plates
- Yellow paint
- Brushes
- Gold yarn cut in 2″ lengths
- Precut facial features
- Paste

Procedure:

1. After discussing the zoo with the children, talk about the lion in more detail. Explain that the male lion has a mane (lots of thick hair) around its neck and shoulders.
2. Hold up a paper plate and talk about its shape (a circle). Have each child trace around the rim of his or her plate to "feel" a circle.
3. Have the children paint their plates yellow. When the plates are almost dry, help the children arrange the facial features on the lion.
4. Help each child spread paste around the rim of the painted plate, making a layer of paste about 1″ thick.
5. Have the children glue the yarn pieces all around the rim to make the lion's mane.

Variations/Ways to Extend:

- Cut out the lion's eyes and mouth from the painted plate and glue a tongue depressor to the bottom of the plate to make a stick mask.
- Read *Sam Who Never Forgets* by Eve Rice (New York: Greenwillow, 1977).

I-131   CIRCUS TRAIN

Subject Area: Music

Concepts/Skills: Listens to a simple song
Repeats parts of a song

Objectives: The children will listen and move to a song about the circus.

Materials: • Words and music to the song "Circus Train"
• Pictures of circus scenes

Procedure:

1. Show pictures of the circus, pointing out clowns, various acts, animals, the audience, and so on.
2. Teach the song "Circus Train" and repeat it several times so the children become familiar with it.
3. Let the children form a train by holding on to one another's waist as they move around the room singing the song.

Variations/Ways to Extend:

• If possible, visit a circus or invite a clown or other circus personnel to visit the school. Introduce the visitor by playing the record "The Clown" on *Pretend* by Hap Palmer (Educational Activities, Inc., Box 392, Freeport, N.Y. 11520).
• Make up the children's faces with nontoxic clown makeup. Then throw several balloons into the air and let the children try to prevent them from touching the floor.

Circus Train

Words and Music by BOB MESSANO
Arranged by John Sheehan

2. Ding! Ding! Ding!
3. Chug-a-chug chug!
4. Toot! Toot! Toot!

Weekly Subtheme: The Circus and Circus Animals

I-132 FISHING FOR ANIMALS

Subject Area: Language Arts

Concepts/Skills: Distinguishes between "big" and "little"
Knows the names of three animals

Objective: The children will distinguish between big and little circus animals.

Materials:
- Pictures of adult and baby circus animals
- Yarn 2′ long
- Magnet
- Paper clips
- Cardboard
- Glue
- String

Procedure:

1. Mount pictures of elephants, bears, horses, lions, tigers, and seals onto cardboard. Be sure each card shows an adult animal and its baby.
2. Discuss the words "big" and "little" and point out appropriate objects in the room that fit those descriptions.
3. Now place two paper clips on each picture.
4. Tell the children about the "three rings of the circus" while making a ring from a circle of yarn on the floor.
5. Put all the animal pictures inside the circus ring.
6. Tie a magnet onto a piece of string and let each child "fish" for a picture.
7. Help the child identify the animal and point to which is big and which is little.

Variation/Way to Extend:

- Let the children pretend to be lions as they jump through a hula hoop onto big pillows or a soft mat.

Weekly Subtheme: The Circus and Circus Animals

I–133 PAPER ELEPHANT

Subject Area: Art

Concepts/Skills: Applies glue
Explores new materials
Paints with a large brush

Objective: The children will construct an elephant from paper.

Materials:
- Large white sheets of paper cut into ovals
- Pipe cleaners
- Gray paint
- Paintbrushes
- Precut head (with ear) and legs from gray construction paper
- Books and pictures of elephants
- Glue
- Hole puncher

Procedure:

1. Show several books and pictures of elephants to the children.
2. Let the children paint their paper ovals gray and allow them to dry.
3. Then paste the elephant's head to the left top part of the oval, paste on the legs, and push a pipe cleaner through prepunched holes to make a trunk and a tail.
4. Demonstrate how elephants walk in the circus (each elephant uses its trunk to hold the tail of the elephant in front of it) and how they stand on their hind legs and roll over.

Variation/Way to Extend:
- Read *The Circus* by Brian Wildsmith (New York: Oxford University Press, 1970.)

I-134   THE ELEPHANT

Subject Area: Language Arts

Concepts/Skills: Repeats parts of a fingerplay
Imitates actions
Counts to three

Objective: The children will participate in a fingerplay about a circus animal.

Materials: • Words to fingerplay (see Procedure section)
• Precut elephant finger puppets.

Procedure:

1. Teach the following fingerplay to the children:
    The elephant has a trunk for a nose (*clasp hands and extend arms*),
    Up and down, that's the way it goes (*raise and lower arms*).
    He wears such a saggy, baggy hide (*relax body*),
    Do you think two elephants would fit inside (*hold up two fingers*)?

2. Have an elephant finger puppet for each child to wear. Show the children how to put their index finger through the hole to make the trunk move.

Variations/Ways to Extend:

• Use finger puppets of other animals and let the children play circus.

• Have a wooden dowel on a stand with three graduated rings placed on it. Use the rings to talk about the three rings of the circus and have the children practice stacking them by size.

I–135 PEANUT THROW

Subject Area: Gross Motor Games

Concept/Skill: Throws a small object two feet

Objective: The children will throw peanuts to "feed" the elephant.

Materials:
- Unshelled peanuts
- Large cardboard elephant in a circus outfit
- Masking tape
- Cardboard box

Procedure:

1. Discuss the special tricks elephants do in the circus and show the large picture or drawing of the elephant. Explain that at the zoo or circus, elephants enjoy eating peanuts.
2. Place the elephant picture flat in the cardboard box on the floor.
3. Mark a line on the floor with the masking tape, two feet away from the elephant picture.
4. Give several peanuts to each child.
5. Ask the children to toss the peanuts onto the picture while standing behind the line.

Variation/Way to Extend:

- After the activity, shell some of the peanuts with the children. Then mix with oil and blend in a blender to make homemade peanut butter. Spread the mixture onto crackers and enjoy with milk at snack time.

SPRING

- ○ A New Beginning
- ○ Plant Life
- ○ Air, Rain, and Sunshine
- ○ The Balance of Nature

I-136   FIVE LITTLE FLOWERS

Subject Area: Language Arts

Concepts/Skills: Repeats parts of a fingerplay
Imitates actions
Counts to five

Objectives: The children will learn and recall the words and actions to a fingerplay about spring.

Material: • Words to the fingerplay (see Procedure section)

Procedure:

   1. Teach the children the following fingerplay:

      Five little flowers standing in the sun (*hold up five fingers*).
      See their heads nodding, bowing one by one (*bend fingers one at a time*).
      Down, down, down
      Comes the gentle rain (*raise hands, wiggle fingers, and lower arms*).
      And the five little flowers
      Raise their heads again (*hold up five fingers*).

   2. Let the children try the fingerplay on their own.

Variation/Way to Extend:

   • Make each child a finger ring to wear while saying this fingerplay. Cut a small strip of paper and tape it around the child's finger. Paste a flower picture or cutout to the front of each ring.

I-137 EGGS FOR US!

Subject Area: Nutrition/Foods Experience

Concepts/Skills: Cooperates in a group situation
Learns that matter can change from a liquid to a solid
Follows directions

Objective: The children will participate in a cooking experience where they will help make omelets for snack time.

Materials: (*for every ten children*)
- stove
- 6 eggs
- ½ cup milk
- ½ cup grated mild cheddar cheese
- 2 tablespoons margarine
- Pan
- Spatula
- Bowl
- Eggbeater
- Plates
- Forks
- Napkins

Procedure:

1. Demonstrate how an eggbeater works.
2. Crack the eggs into the bowl and let each child take a turn using the eggbeater.
3. Add the milk and grated cheese.
4. Melt the margarine in the pan and add the egg mixture. (**Caution:** Be sure the children stay away from the stove.)
5. Tell the children to watch as the wet mixture slowly becomes more solid.
6. Use the spatula to lift and turn the eggs over.
7. Serve with milk at snack time.

Variation/Way to Extend:

- For a creative drama experience, have the children role-play baby birds coming out of their eggs. Remind the children that they would be seeing the world for the very first time. Encourage them to tell what they see, hear, and smell.

I-138 MY LITTLE BIRDIE

Subject Area: Music

Concepts/Skills: Participates with pleasure
Develops listening ability
Develops performance ability

Objectives: The children will learn a song about birds and hold up bird pictures while they sing.

Materials:
• Words and music to the song "My Little Birdie"
• Pictures of birds
• Tongue depressors
• Cellophane tape

Procedure:

1. Cut out the bird pictures and tape them onto the tongue depressors.
2. Distribute them to the children. Let the children look at them and hold them up while you teach them the song.

Variations/Ways to Extend:

• Let the children enjoy a movement experience with this song by having them "fly around the room" like birds.
• Teach the children the circle game "Bluebird Through My Window." found in *Singing Bee*, compiled by Jane Hart (New York: Lothrop, Lee and Shepard, 1982).
• Display some of the wonderful, realistic paintings of birds by John James Audubon. Check libraries, bookstores, bird societies, or art distributors for pictures.

My Little Birdie

Words and Music by BOB MESSANO
Arranged by John Sheehan

Presto (♩ = 100)

My lit-tle bird-ie's one day old, She can do what she is told!
Sleep lit-tle bird-ie, sleep, sleep, sleep! Sleep, lil' bird-ie, sleep, sleep, sleep!

2. My little birdie's two days old,
   She can do what she is told!
   Tweet, little birdie,
   Tweet, tweet, tweet!
   Tweet, lil' birdie,
   Tweet, tweet, tweet!

3. My little birdie's three days old,
   She can do what she is told!
   Hop, little birdie,
   Hop, hop, hop!
   Hop, lil' birdie,
   Hop, hop, hop!

4. My little birdie's four days old,
   She can do what she is told!
   Fly, little birdie,
   Fly, fly, fly!
   Fly, lil' birdie,
   Fly, fly, fly!

I–139   SPRING PASTELS

Subject Area: Art

Concepts/Skills: Matches two color samples
Holds chalk

Objectives: The children will use chalk to make pastel pictures and then use these in a matching exercise.

Materials:
- Pastel-colored chalk
- White paper

Procedure:

1. Give each child a piece of pastel-colored chalk such as light green, pink, yellow, or light blue. Be sure that exactly two children are using the same color, that is, only use two pieces of yellow chalk, two of green, and so on.
2. Ask each child to fill up his or her paper as much as possible with chalk drawings.
3. When finished, let each child take a turn finding the other picture that was done in the same color as his or her own.

Variation/Way to Extend:

- For a different experience using colored chalk, wet the paper lightly first and smooth it out on a table. This will give the chalk lines a softer, smoother appearance.

I–140   NESTS

Subject Area: Art

Concepts/Skills: Develops fine motor movements of tearing and pasting
Learns about nests and eggs

Objective: The children will construct a textured nest collage.

Materials:
- Precut paper nest shapes
- Brown paper
- Jute or string
- Precut paper eggs
- Glue
- Pictures of nests (or a real one)

Procedure:

1. Give each child a large piece of paper cut in the general shape of a nest. (See the illustration here for the basic shape.)

2. Let the children tear brown paper into shapes and strips and paste these onto the nest shape.
3. Give the children plenty of jute or string cut in short strips and encourage them to paste these right over their paper strips.
4. Talk to the children about how birds build their nests and what they might use. Show the students pictures of nests or a real one if possible.
5. Then ask the children to paste the precut eggs on top of the nest.

Variations/Ways to Extend:

- Look at the pictures in Millicent Selsam's *All About Eggs* (Reading, Mass.: Addison-Wesley, 1952) and *Egg to Chick* (New York: Harper & Row, Pub., 1970).
- You can also make newspaper nests. Use a double sheet cut in a circle as the bottom. Then fold newspaper into two-inch wide, thick, shallow strips to be used as the sides. Use masking tape to secure the ends and tape the sides to the bottom. Have the children mold eggs from flour dough and place them in the nests on a bed of straw.
- Go outside and see if the children can locate any nests. Be sure the children do not disturb any inhabited ones!

I-141 SEEDS

Subject Area: Language Arts

Concept/Skill: Repeats parts of a fingerplay

Objective: The children will demonstrate the actions of the fingerplay.

Materials:
- Words to the fingerplay (see Procedure section)
- Milkweed pods with fluff (if available)

Procedure:

1. Teach the children the following words and actions:

   In a milkweed cradle (*cup hands*)
   Snug and warm
   Baby seeds are hiding (*make self small*)
   Safe from harm.
   Open wide the cradle (*open hands*)
   Hold it high.
   Come, Mr. Wind (*blow in hands*),
   Make them fly.

2. Repeat the fingerplay several times so the children become familiar with it.

Variation/Way to Extend:

- Tell the children to listen for the "magic word" in this fingerplay. (The word "seeds" is the one you will be concentrating on this week, so this gives the children the opportunity to focus on a specific topic.)

Weekly Subtheme: Plant Life

I-142 PLANTING SEEDS

Subject Area: Science

Concepts/Skills: Develops observation ability
Develops inquisitiveness

Objectives: The children will observe and describe the experience of growing a plant from a seed.

Materials:
- Clear plastic cups
- Potting soil
- Lima beans
- Markers
- Pebbles for drainage
- Water

Procedures:

1. First, soak the beans in water overnight.
2. The next day, have the children put a few pebbles in the bottom of a plastic cup.
3. Then have them add about 2″ of soil and place a few lima beans on top. Cover with more soil and water lightly. (Lima beans are suggested because of their quick germination period, rapid growth, and large easy-to-detect seedlings.)
4. Label each cup with the child's name and place it in a sunny window.
5. Have the children observe these daily and participate in watering them. Encourage them to ask questions.
6. When the seedlings are a few inches tall, transplant them into a school garden or send them home for the families to enjoy.
7. In addition to this activity, it is also exciting to take a few of those soaked lima beans, open them up, and let the children see the "baby plant" growing on the inside.

Variation/Way to Extend:

- Secure an 11″ by 14″ color reproduction of "A Girl with a Watering Can" by Auguste Renoir (No. 1870) from the National Gallery of Art, Publications Service, Washington, D.C. 20565. Write for current prices and any handling charges.

Weekly Subtheme: Plant Life

I-143   STRAWBERRY TARTS

Subject Area: Nutrition/Foods Experience

Concepts/Skills: Measures ingredients
Sees how matter changes from a liquid to a solid
Follows directions

Objectives: The children will enjoy a spring fruit by helping to prepare a recipe and eating the finished product.

Materials: (*for every six students*)
- 1 quart strawberries
- Prebaked tart shells
- ½ cup honey
- ½ cup water
- ⅓ cup heavy cream
- Beater
- Bowl
- Knife
- Saucepan
- Stove
- Spoons
- Measuring cup

Procedure:

1. Right before snack time, let the children wash and drain the strawberries. Then you slice them lengthwise.
2. Just prior to serving, help the children arrange the strawberries in the tart shells.
3. Meanwhile, boil the honey and water until syrupy. (**Caution:** Be sure the children do not go near the heat.)
4. Beat the heavy cream until whipped and thick, letting the children see how the cream changes from a liquid to a more solid state.
5. Pour the honey and water syrup over the berries, garnish with the whipped cream, and serve at once for a delicious snack.

Variations/Ways to Extend:

- If the children are celebrating a special occasion, make this recipe to add a wonderful festive touch to the party.
- For background music during this snack, play a recording of "Garden of Live Flowers" (Through the Looking Glass Suite) by Deems Taylor. It is found in the *Adventures in Music* series available from RCA Records, P.O. Box RCA 1000, Indianapolis, Ind. 46291.

Weekly Subtheme: Plant Life

I–144 SPRING GARDENING

Subject Area: Math

Concepts/Skills: Counts two objects
Associates common objects with use

Objective: The children will count up to two objects while observing items associated with gardening.

Materials: • Flannelboard
• Felt shapes—matched pairs of gardening items

Procedure:

1. Cut pairs of gardening items from felt. Examples would be two flowerpots, plants, flowers, spades, rakes, watering cans, and leaves.
2. Gather the children in a group and explain the process of planting.
3. As you place each item on the flannelboard, have the children count them out loud, "one, two, flowerpots" and, "one, two watering cans."
4. Continue with the others and help the children to count the objects.
5. Talk about how each object is used and have the children express their ideas about usage.

Variation/Way to Extend:

• Read *The Tiny Seed* by Eric Carle (New York: Thomas Y. Crowell, 1970).

I-145 PEEK-A-BOO

Subject Area: Music

Concepts/Skills: Participates with enthusiasm
Listens to melody and words

Objectives: The children will listen to a song about a garden and accompany the words with actions.

Material: • Words and music to the song "Peek-a-Boo"

Procedure:

1. Teach the children the song "Peek-a-Boo."
2. Invite the children to act out the actions mentioned in the last line of each verse.
3. See if the children can mention other plants or animals found in a garden and portray these actions as well.

Variations/Ways to Extend:

• Teach the nursery rhyme "Mary, Mary, Quite Contrary." Instruct the children to play musical bells during the last two lines of the verse.

Mary, Mary, quite contrary,
How does your garden grow?
With silver bells and cockle shells
And pretty maids all in a row.

• Use "Mary, Mary, Quite Contrary" for a pantomime experience in which each child who wants to can act out the role of Mary. Let the children relate the role of the character in their own way.

Peek-a-Boo

Words and Music by BOB MESSANO
Arranged by John Sheehan

Moderato (♩ = 120)

1. Peek - a - boo, I see you! Bird - ie in the gar - den.

Peek - a - boo, what shall we do? Let us fly in the gar - den!

2. Peek-a-boo, I see you!
   Rabbit in the garden.
   Peek-a-boo, what shall we do?
   Let us hop in the garden!

3. Peek-a-boo, I see you!
   Spider in the garden.
   Peek-a-boo, what shall we do?
   Let us crawl in the garden!

4. Peek-a-boo, I see you!
   Flower in the graden.
   Peek-a-boo, what shall we do?
   Let us grow in the garden!

I-146 WHERE'S THE PUDDLE?

Subject Area: Science

Concepts/Skills: Compares differences
Notices effects of wet and dry

Objectives: The children will observe that rain creates puddles and that the passage of time and the sunshine will cause evaporation.

Materials: • An outdoor area with a hard surface
• Chalk

Procedure:

1. After it rains, take the children on a walk to find a nearby puddle.
2. Bring along some chalk and trace the outline of the puddle on the ground.
3. Talk about how the rainfall collected in that particular space.
4. Return to the location several hours later if it's sunny or the next day, and trace the puddle again. Point out the distance between the lines and how this shows that the puddle became much smaller because the water changed into a mist and went up into the air.

Variation/Way to Extend:

• Read *Pete's Puddle* by Joanna Foster and Beatrice Darwin (San Diego: Harcourt Brace Jovanovich, 1969).

I-147 A SUNNY, BOUNCY DAY

Subject Area: Gross Motor Games

Concepts/Skills: Throws a small object two feet
Catches a rolled ball
Rolls a ball forward
Understands the idea of waiting one's turn
Learns about roundness

Objectives: The children will identify the sun as round and will play some rolling and throwing games outdoors.

Materials:
- Large open area outdoors
- Large rubber ball
- Chalk
- Beanbag

Procedure:

1. Discuss the idea that everyone needs fresh air and sunshine to be healthy and to grow. Compare sunny areas to shady areas.
2. Talk about the sun being round and look for other objects that are round. Let the children suggest a ball.
3. Take a large ball outside and have each child take a turn rolling it forward. Demonstrate how to hold it still on the ground and then give it a little push forward with the hands.
4. Let the children take turns retrieving the ball for one another.
5. Next, draw a chalk line. Then 2' away and parallel to this one, draw another line.
6. Let each child take a turn standing behind the first chalk line and throwing a small beanbag so that it lands on or passes the other line.

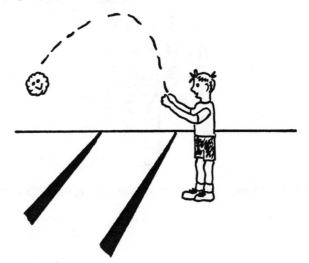

Variations/Ways to Extend:

- Let the children paint large, bright yellow suns at the easels.
- Prepare hard-boiled eggs (peel ahead of time) and let the children enjoy them as a snack outdoors. Let the children discover the round yellow yolk in each egg.

I–148 SUNSHINE FLOWERS

Subject Area: Art

Concepts/Skills: Recalls that the sun gives light
Identifies the sun
Develops fine motor movement of taping

Objectives: The children will construct paper flowers and observe the effect of sunshine on them.

Materials:
- Precut petals of red, yellow, and blue cellophane
- Construction paper circles, 1″ diameter
- ½″ by 4″ green oaktag strips
- Cellophane tape
- Scissors

Procedure:

1. Assist the children in taping the flower center (paper circle) to the oaktag stem (strip) and then the petals to the center.
2. Encourage the children to hold these flowers up to the sunlight coming through a window. Do they see how pretty the light looks shining through their flowers?
3. Let the children know that they can either take their flowers home or decorate the room by taping them in front of the windows, where they can enjoy the sunshine as it filters through the petals during the day.

Variations/Ways to Extend:

- Let the children arrange the colored petals so that they overlap slightly, allowing the secondary colors to be created.

- Show the children that by overlapping all the colors, black is produced.

I–149 'EENSY-WEENSY SPIDER

Subject Area: Language Arts

Concepts/Skills: Listens to words
Repeats parts of a fingerplay
Imitates actions

Objective: The children will participate in a fingerplay about a spider in the rain.

Material: • Words to the fingerplay (see Procedure section)

Procedure:

1. Teach the children the following popular fingerplay:

    The 'eensy-weensy spider went up the waterspout
    (*put thumb and index finger together on both hands, allow fingers of both hands to touch, and make a winding motion going up*).
    Down came the rain and washed the spider out
    (*wiggle all fingers in a downward motion*).
    Out came the sun and dried up all the rain
    (*make a circle of both arms overhead*).
    And the 'eensy-weensy spider went up the spout again
    (*repeat motion for first line*).

2. Repeat the fingerplay several times.

Variations/Ways to Extend:

• Speak to the children about how spiders are helpful since they eat flies and other unhealthful insects.
• Observe the different kinds of clouds that appear in the sky. What do the shapes look like? When it rains, listen to the sound of rain hitting the roof. Have the children make rain sounds with their hands: gentle clapping, rubbing hands together, and gently tapping on the table.

I-150 CATCHING BUBBLES!

Subject Area: Science

Concepts/Skills: Develops ability to observe, describe, and compare
Develops fine motor movements of mixing and blowing

Objective: The children will conclude that bubbles are made of soapy water and air.

Materials:
- Commercial bubble mixture *or* beat together with eggbeater in a bowl: ½ cup dishwashing liquid, ¼ cup glycerine, 2½ cups water, and a pinch of sugar
- Bubble wand
- Plastic dishes
- Feathers
- Strips of paper

Procedure:

1. Talk to the children about the air we breathe, how it goes in through our noses, into our lungs, and comes out of our mouths when we blow.
2. Let them blow against their hands, a tiny feather, a strip of paper, and a cold window.
3. Let the children help to prepare the bubble mixture, especially the mixing of ingredients using an eggbeater.
4. With the wand, make bubbles for the children to catch. Let them notice how the soapy water forms a round shell and that you are blowing air into it to make bubbles.
5. Point out shapes, colors, flat edges, and the fact that the bubbles can be seen through.
6. Distribute some small plastic dishes and pour a little soapy water into each.
7. Let the children use the dishes to catch the bubbles you make. The bubbles will remain intact for a short time if caught on the soapy dishes.

Variations/Ways to Extend:

- Take the bubble mixture outdoors and observe the wind blowing the bubbles away. Use sheets of cardboard to fan air at the bubbles and make them go in different directions.
- Let the children blow bubbles with the wands or in deep pans with meat basters.
- Read the following poem by Robert Louis Stevenson to the children:

THE SWING

How do you like to go up in a swing,
  Up in the air so blue?
Oh, I do think it is the pleasantest thing
  Ever a child can do!

Up in the air and over the wall,
  Till I can see so wide,
Rivers and trees and cattle and all
  Over the countryside—

Till I look down on the garden green,
  Down on the roof so brown—
Up in the air I go flying again,
  Up in the air and down!

I-151   A SENSE WALK

Subject Area: Science

Concepts/Skills: Begins to develop senses
Associates grass, plants, and trees with correct objects

Objectives: The children will observe and describe the elements of nature.

Material: • Large outdoor area

Procedure:

1. Take a short walk on a lovely spring day and focus the children's interests on their five senses.
2. Using the sense of sight, look for the bright colors of spring (the sky, grass, trees, flowers), notice textures (smooth grass, rough bark), compare sizes of rocks, trees, bushes, or animals, and look for birds and note their colors and movements.
3. Using the sense of touch, experience various shapes, textures, and weights.
4. Using the sense of hearing, compare natural sounds to man-made sounds in the environment. Encourage the children's language to describe what they are "sensing."
5. Using the sense of smell, let the children appreciate the scent of freshly cut grass, flowers in bloom, the bark of a tree, and a wet rock.
6. You might even be lucky enough to use the sense of taste by enjoying some fresh local berries or early fruits or vegetables.

Variation/Way to Extend:

• Bring a small paper bag for each child to use in collecting found objects on their walk. Upon returning to the classroom, encourage them to examine the objects with a small magnifying glass, and compare sizes, shapes, hardness, and colors.

I-152 RAINBOW COLORS

Subject Area: Art

Concepts/Skills: Matches colors
Develops fine motor control

Objectives: The children will be introduced to the word "rainbow" and make paper rainbows.

Materials:
• Colored tissue paper
• Clear, self-stick vinyl
• Cellophane tape
• Scissors
• String

Procedure:

1. Cover colored tissue paper sheets with clear, self-stick vinyl.
2. Cut out rainbow arches from the laminated tissue paper.
3. Allow the children to select the colors they want for their rainbows.
4. Help the children tape the arches onto a length of string.
5. Hang the rainbows from the classroom windows.

Variations/Ways to Extend:

• Create a real outdoor rainbow. On a sunny day, turn your back to the sun and spray a water hose in a fine mist.
• Put a mirror in a glass of water and place it on a sunny windowsill. The caught light will create a rainbow.
• Give prisms to the children for them to have fun with.

I-153   COUNTING NATURE MATERIALS

Subject Area: Math

Concepts/Skills: Indicates awareness of more than two
Groups things together

Objectives: The children will be able to demonstrate rote counting of three objects.

Materials: • Three grouping of five different types of nature materials, such as three leaves, three stones, three twigs, three seeds, and three flowers.

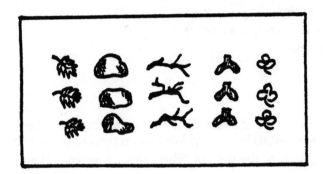

Procedure:

1. Start with the three leaves, for example, and say, "Look at these pretty leaves. Let's find out how many we have by counting them." Place the three leaves five inches apart and count from left to right.
2. Encourage each child to use his or her index finger and touch each leaf while counting (with your help if necessary). Be sure to praise each child.
3. Remove the leaves and display the next grouping of three nature materials.
4. Continue the counting from left to right.

Variation/Way to Extend:

• Teach the children the following fingerplay:

Hickory dickory dock,
The mouse ran up the clock (*fingers run up child's body*),
The clock struck one (*count one and clap*),
The mouse ran down (*fingers run down child's body*),
Hickory dickory dock.

Weekly Subtheme: The Balance of Nature

I-154   FLY AWAY BIRDS

Subject Area: Language Arts

Concepts/Skills: Names pictured objects
Repeats parts of a rhyme
Jumps with two feet together
Follows simple rules in a game

Objectives: The children will be able to identify a bird, move like birds, and repeat a four-line rhyme.

Materials:
- Pictures of birds
- Seeds, such as sesame seeds
- Masking tape
- Feeding tray

Procedure:

1. Show the children a picture of a bird. Say, "This is a picture of a bird. Birds like to eat seeds. (Show sesame seeds.) Birds like to fly. We can pretend to fly like this." (Flap arms.)

2. Sing the following song to the tune of "Row, Row, Row your Boat":

   Fly, fly, fly away
   Cheerful as can be.
   Fly, fly, fly away
   Then fly home to me.

3. Have each child, one at a time, fly away to the other side of the room and back to you while repeating the rhyme.

4. Place four strips of tape on the floor to form a square. Say, "We are going to pretend this is a nest." Ask the students to jump into and out of the nest.

5. Conclude the lesson by explaining to the children the importance of being nice to birds and feeding them seeds. Ask the children what they like about birds, and why they think we should be kind to them.

6. Have the children go outside and sprinkle the seeds on a feeding tray set at eye level for the birds to eat. You might have the children make "birdy" sounds (tweet, tweet) while sprinkling the seeds.

Variations/Ways to Extend:

- Spread peanut butter onto apple slices and have the children sprinkle sesame seeds on top. Let the children enjoy this snack with juice.
- Read the following poem to the children:

ONCE I SAW A LITTLE BIRD
Once I saw a little bird
Come hop, hop, hop;
So I cried, "Little bird,
Will you stop, stop, stop?"

And I was going to the window,
To say, "How do you do?"
But he shook his little tail
And far away he flew.

—*Anonymous*

I-155   NATURE COLLAGE

Subject Area: Art

Concepts/Skills: Associates words with objects
Develops fine motor movements of applying glue and pasting

Objective: The children will be able to construct nature collages.

Materials:
- Nature materials
- Tagboard squares
- Glue

Procedure:

1. Place several nature materials (leaves, twigs, grass, pebbles, flowers, and weeds) onto a table. Say, "Look at all these pieces we've gathered on our walk. All of them come from nature— from the trees, grass, and bushes." Associate the fact that leaves and twigs come from trees.
2. Identify the pieces and have the children repeat each name.
3. Tell the children they are going to make a beautiful picture using the items found outside.
4. Provide the children with paper and glue. Demonstrate how to apply the glue to each item and then press it onto the paper.
5. Allow the children to choose their own nature items. Praise their work, specifying the colors used or the way things were put together, or how the items fill the page.

Variations/Ways to Extend:

- Read the Caldecott Honor book *The Happy Day* by Ruth Krauss (New York: Harper & Row, Pub., 1949).
- Listen to "Black-Eyed Susan" on *Songs of Nature and the Environment* by G. Axelrod and R. Macklin (Folkways Records, 632 Broadway, New York. N.Y. 10012).

COMMUNITY WORKERS

- ○ Health Professionals—

  Doctors, Nurses, Dentists

- ○ Police Officers and Firefighters

- ○ Shopkeepers and Office Workers

- ○ Librarians and Postal Workers

I-156   LISTEN TO MY HEARTBEAT

Subject Area: Science

Concepts/Skills: Obtains idea of a heartbeat
Associates medical instrument with use
Indicates awareness of more than two

Objective: The children will listen to their own heartbeats and those of others.

Materials: • Real stethoscope

Procedure:

1. Borrow a stethoscope to allow the children the very concrete experience of listening to heartbeats. The exposure to a real medical instrument might lessen anxiety the next time they visit their doctors. They can listen to their own heartbeats, those of their classmates, and also those of a classroom pet, such as a friendly gerbil. How are they the same? Different?

2. Let a child count two heartbeats. Now have him or her run around the room or jump in place and listen to his or her heart again. See if he or she notices that the beat is faster as well as louder this time. The children will understand that their heart beats faster after exercise. Explain why this is good for them. "When our heart beats fast, our blood travels fast and helps our bodies grow strong."

Variation/Way to Extend

• As a musical or fingerplay extension, teach "Where Is Thumbkin?" and stress the idea of being "very well, I thank you."

I–157   ORANGES AND GRAPEFRUITS

Subject Area: Nutrition/Foods Experience

Concepts/Skills: Begins to develop sense of touch, taste, smell, and sight
Understands concept of one
Understands whole and half, same and different, sweet and sour

Objective: The children will compare the attributes of a grapefruit and an orange.

Materials:
- Grapefruits
- Oranges
- Knife
- Cutting board
- Paper plates

Procedure:

1. Discuss with the children the idea of staying healthy by eating good foods, resting, sleeping, and exercising. Talk about fruits as being a group of foods that are good for us.
2. Show the children one orange and one grapefruit. Let them observe the differences in size and color and the similarity in shape. Ask the children to close their eyes and encourage them to feel the skin textures of both.
3. Cut each fruit in half and have the children note the scent of each, the number and size of the seeds inside, and any other traits that make them similar and different as well.
4. Serve the orange and grapefruit slices for a snack. Let the children compare the two tastes (sweet and sour).

Variations/Ways to Extend:

- Demonstrate the making of juice from these two fruits by using an electric or hand-held juicer. Serve the freshly squeezed juices at snack time.
- Display an 11″ by 14″ art reproduction of "Still Life" (No. 1810) by Henri Fantin-Latour from the National Gallery of Art, Publications Service, Washington, D.C. 20565. Write for current prices and any handling charges.

I-158   MEDICAL COLLAGE

Subject Area: Art

Concepts/Skills: Explores various textures and materials
Matches parts to the whole
Associates use with common objects

Objective: The children will construct a collage of items associated with medicine.

Materials: • Medical and/or dental toy kits
• Scissors
• Paper
• Paste
• Gauze
• Adhesive tape
• Bandaids
• Cotton
• Tongue depressors
• Orange sticks

Procedure:

1. Allow the children some dramatic play time with the medical or dental toy kits.
2. Cut up the materials into pieces and see if the children can match them to the whole items they had in their kits.
3. Distribute the paste and paper and guide the children in making collages using the cut-up materials.

Variation/Way to Extend:

• Show pictures or posters of medical and dental personnel using the materials in situations with children, such as giving checkups or treating wounds. Be sure to show both sexes in the roles of these professionals.

I-159 DOCTORS' TOOLS

Subject Area: Language Arts

Concepts/Skills: Enjoys looking at books
Matches pictured objects
Places objects *on* the flannelboard

Objective: The children will engage in a flannelboard activity about medical tools.

Materials:
- Flannelboard
- Felt patterns
- Fabric glue
- Book
- Scissors

Procedure:

1. Cut out the patterns on the next page. Trace the patterns onto felt and glue the felt outlines to their backs.
2. Read *Doctors' Tools* by Marguerite R. Lerner (Minneapolis, Minn.: Lerner, 1960) to the children and have them select the flannel pattern that is depicted as the story is read.
3. Ask a child to place each piece of equipment on the flannelboard as it is mentioned.
4. Discuss the use of each piece of equipment to help the children's understanding.

Variations/Ways to Extend:

- Listen to the album *Learning Basic Skills Through Music: Health and Safety* by Hap Palmer, especially "Keep the Germs Away" and "Cover Your Mouth" (Educational Activities, Freeport, N.Y. 11520).
- Invite a doctor (preferably a woman to help counteract stereotypes) to share her tools with the children.

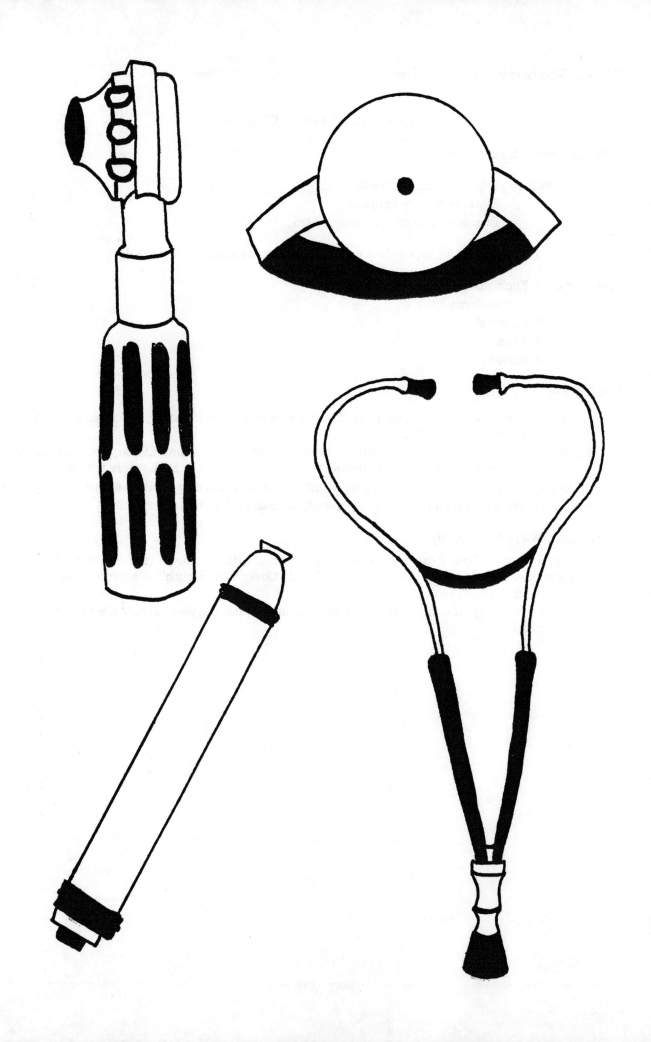

I–160   CLEAN TEETH

Subject Area: Science

Concepts/Skills: Develops self-care
Brushes teeth

Objective: The children will practice brushing their teeth.

Materials:
- A new toothbrush for each child
- Little tube of toothpaste for each (possibly secured as samples)
- Little paper cups (for rinsing)

Procedure:

1. Children's teeth are prone to decay; therefore a real experience in preventive dental care is appropriate. Have a "learning by doing" activity by labeling new, small toothbrushes with each child's name and distributing these along with little tubes of toothpaste to each child.

2. Assist the children in squeezing the proper amount of toothpaste on a brush and allow them to manage brushing and rinsing for themselves. You might demonstrate correct brushing technique if necessary.

3. The brushes and paste may go home with the children, where they may serve as a reminder to parents that their children are not too young to develop sound dental habits. Or they may be kept at school to be used by the children after meals.

Variations/Ways to Extend:

- Give the children small flashlights to inspect one another's teeth or to look into the mouths of the dolls in the room.
- Show the pictures in *How Many Teeth?* by Paul Showers (New York: Harper & Row, Pub., 1976) and briefly paraphrase the story for the children.

I-161   FIRE PRINT HATS

Subject Area: Art

Concepts/Skills: Paints with a large brush
Develops exploration ability

Objective: The children will create paintings on firefighter-style hats.

Materials: • 12″ by 18″ white construction paper
• Scissors
• Red and yellow paint
• Paintbrushes

Procedure:

1. Cut the white paper into large oval shapes.
2. Help each child fold a sheet in half, with the twelve-inch-long edges touching.
3. Unfold and let the children use their brushes to drip red and yellow paint over one-half of the paper.
4. Fold on the same fold again and gently press and smooth the paper. Open the papers up and discuss what happened to the colors and the "firey" look they have.
5. When the papers are dry, cut a hole approximately five inches across and six inches at the highest point in the center of the paper to fit each child's head. They can wear their firefighter hats to engage in dramatic play. Be sure to mention that we have women and men firefighters.

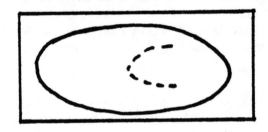

Variations/Ways to Extend:

• Let the children sort red and yellow objects into two boxes lined with those colors, respectively.
• Borrow a real firefighter hat from your local station so that the children can see it and try it on.

I-162   THE FIREFIGHTERS

Subject Area: Language Arts

Concepts/Skills: Imitates actions
                      Repeats parts of a fingerplay

Objective: The children will participate in a fingerplay about firefighters.

Material: • Words to the fingerplay (see Procedure section)

Procedure:

1. Demonstrate the following fingerplay to the children:

> Ten brave firefighters (*ten fingers, straight up*)
> Sleeping in a row (*fingers are out flat*).
> Ding goes the bell (*clap hands*),
> Down the pole they go (*hands go down imaginary pole*),
> Jumping on the engine (*make driving motions*)
> Putting out the fire (*pretend to hold hose*)
> Drive home—go slow (*driving motion—slow*)
> Back to bed again (*hands form pillow*)
> All in a row (*fingers are out flat*).

2. Repeat the fingerplay several times with the children.

Variation/Way to Extend:

• Read *The Little Fireman* by Margaret W. Brown (Reading, Mass.: Addison-Wesley, 1952).

I–163   POLICE VEST AND BADGE

Subject Area: Social Studies

Concepts/Skills: Paints with a large brush
Uses scissors to cut paper
Applies glue

Objectives: The children will construct and paint a police officer's vest and badge.

Materials:
- One large paper bag per child
- One index card per child
- Yellow paint
- Blue paint
- Paintbrushes
- Newspapers
- Picture of a police officer
- Scissors
- Marker
- Glue

Procedure:

1. Show a picture of a police officer and have a discussion on how he or she helps us. Point out the uniform and badge.
2. Help the children cut a neck hole and two arm holes in each paper bag by having the open end face you and positioning the holes on the opposite side.
3. Assist the children in cutting a slit up the front of the bag.
4. Lay the bags on the newspaper-covered table and have the children paint the outside of the bags blue (for a blue uniform).
5. Then have the children paint the index cards yellow. When the cards are dry, cut them into star shapes for badges.
6. Label each badge with a different child's name and let the children paste their name badges onto their own vests.

Variation/Way to Extend:
- Look at the pictures in *I Want to Be a Policeman* by Carla Greene (Chicago: Childrens Press, 1958).

I–164 MY FIRE ENGINE!

Subject Area: Art

Concepts/Skills: Explores colors
Expresses creatively
Develops finger strength and dexterity.

Objective: The children will create a finger painting on a fire engine shape.

Materials:
- Precut large fire engine shapes from finger-paint paper or glossy shelf paper
- Red paint
- Orange paint
- Cellophane tape

Procedure:

1. Tape each precut fire engine shape to a table.
2. Allow the children to freely explore the red and orange paints as they cover their fire engines with their own designs.

Variation/Way to Extend:

- If possible, invite the local fire department's personnel to drive an engine to the school to give the children a first-hand observational experience. Or arrange for a visit to the fire station.

I-165 THE FIRE SONG

Subject Area: Music

Concepts/Skills: Participates in a group
Plays using symbols
Repeats simple songs

Objective: The children will participate in a song about the job of the firefighter.

Materials:
- Words and music to "The Fire Song."
- Bells
- Fire hats
- Wooden crates or cardboard boxes for fire trucks

Procedure:

1. Teach the children "The Fire Song" and encourage them to sing along.
2. Have the children act out the words to the song with the bells, hats, and "firetrucks."

Variation/Way to Extend:

- Tape-record yourself and the children singing this song and play it for them when they are on the climbing equipment (ladder and slide). They can pretend they are on a fire engine or coming down the pole in the firehouse.

The Fire Song

Words and Music by BOB MESSANO
Arranged by John Sheehan

(Chorus)
2. Who will go up the ladder
   And put out a great big fire?
   Let's all go up the ladder
   And put out a great big fire!

(Chorus)
3. Who will hold the fire hose
   And put out a great big fire?
   Let's all hold the fire hose
   And put out a great big fire!

(Chorus)
4. Who will go down the pole
   And put out a great big fire?
   Let's all go down the pole
   And put out a great big fire!

I–166 CLOTHING STORE

Subject Area: Social Studies

Concepts/Skills: Puts on and removes clothes unassisted
Labels items of clothing

Objectives: The children will practice putting on and taking off clothes.

Materials:
- Children's clothes
- Doughnut-shaped cereal
- Thin licorice strips

Procedure:

1. Let the children pretend they are shopping in a clothing store. Set aside the discarded clothes or dramatic play clothing in a certain space in the room.
2. Let the children practice putting the clothes on, zipping up and down, and taking simple items off by themselves. Ask them to name each piece of clothing as they use it.
3. To make a jewelry display for the "store," have the children string the doughnut-shaped cereal onto thin licorice strips to make necklaces and bracelets.

Variation/Way to Extend:

- Make available an assortment of clothing pictures cut from catalogs. Let the children paste some pictures onto paper to make a "store window."

I-167   LET'S PAINT THE SCHOOL!

Subject Area: Creative Dramatics/Movement

Concepts/Skills: Develops role-play ability
Develops gross motor movements of walking up and down stairs alone
Describes what happened in a few words

Objective: The children will demonstrate the role of the house painter.

Materials:
- Painter caps
- Work shirts
- Plastic pails
- Large paintbrushes
- Wooden stirrers
- Paint rollers
- Rolling trays
- Paint pads and holders
- Newspapers
- Water
- Child-sized stepping stool

Procedure:

1. Collect as many of the items listed above as possible. The painter caps can often be obtained free at paint stores, and work shirts could be adult shirts cut down to child size. The rolling trays could be flat shirt boxes with one end flap cut off.
2. Go outdoors on a lovely spring day.
3. Help the children organize their equipment and space themselves apart. Let them "paint" the school building with their "paint cans" of water.
4. Use the stepping stool to have them paint "high" places.
5. After the painting session has ended, encourage the children to describe in a few words how they felt and what happened.

Variation/Way to Extend:

- Use a puppet figure representing a house painter to have another discussion about this experience two days later. Encourage as much recall as possible from the children.

I-168 PRODUCT COLLAGE WINDOW

Subject Area: Language Arts

Concepts/Skills: Points to common objects on command
Groups things together
Applies glue

Objectives: The children will identify items and construct a collage of pictures.

Materials: • Lunch-sized paper bags
• Precut magazine and catalog pictures of foods, toys, and furniture
• Glue

Procedure:

1. Prepare the bags by cutting a large rectangle from one side of the bag.
2. Discuss the pictures with the children. What are they? How are they alike? How are they different?
3. Have the children sort the pile of pictures into categories and then choose the one they would like to use to make a collage. For example, a child could choose products of the toy store.
4. Help the children paste their pictures on the inside of the paper bags so that they show through the cutout side.

Variations/Ways to Extend:

• Teach the nursery rhymes "To market, to market, to buy a fat pig" and "This little pig went to market."
• Read *The First Book of Supermarkets* by Jeanne Bendick (New York: Watts, 1954).

Weekly Subtheme: Shopkeepers and Office Workers

I-169 PIZZA SHOP

Subject Area: Nutrition/Foods Experience

Concepts/Skills: Begins to develop senses of touch, smell, and taste
Develops fine motor movements of rolling, pinching, and spooning
Learns about the idea of a shop

Objectives: The children will make individual pizzas and play Pizza Restaurant.

Materials:
- Ingredients for Quick Pizza Dough (see below)
- Tomato sauce
- Shredded mozzarella cheese
- Parmesan cheese
- Oregano and basil
- Cookie sheets
- Rolling pins
- Oven
- Paper plates
- Spoons
- Play money

Procedure:

1. Talk to the children about eating pizza with their families.
2. Make Quick Pizza Dough following this recipe:

   Sift together 3 cups unbleached white flour, 2 teaspoons sugar, and 1½ teaspoons salt.
   Dissolve 4 teaspoons dry yeast in 2 tablespoons warm water.
   Add ½ cup lukewarm water and ½ cup lukewarm milk to the yeast in the water.
   Add 3 tablespoons melted butter and stir into the yeast mixture.
   Add the yeast mixture to the flour mixture and blend until smooth.
   Knead into a ball. Cover with a cloth and let stand in a warm place for 15 minutes.
   Knead for 10 minutes more and divide into pieces.
   Let the children roll, stretch, and form the dough into small, round biscuit shapes.
   Set aside these pieces and let rise for several minutes.

3. Let each child put his or her dough biscuit on the cookie sheet, spoon tomato sauce on top, and sprinkle with mozzarella cheese. Add a little Parmesan cheese and a pinch of basil and oregano to each.
4. Bake at 350° F for about 20 minutes or until the mozzarella melts. (**Caution:** Be sure the children stay away from the hot oven.)
5. Give the children some paper plates and play money and let them serve each other pizza in their Pizza Restaurant.

Variation/Way to Extend:

- Make this activity more attractive by adding a tablecloth, napkins, flatware, and cups. Allow the children to serve one another in restaurant style.

I–170   BAKER'S HAT

Subject Area: Art

Concepts/Skills: Learns about the idea of a hat
Develops fine motor movements of folding, pasting, crumpling, rolling, pounding, and squeezing

Objectives: The children will construct bakers' hats and role-play being bakers.

Materials:
- White construction paper
- White tissue paper
- Cellophane Tape
- Glue
- Flour dough
- Bowls
- Stapler

- Cookie cutters
- Rolling pins
- Cookie sheets
- Cake pans
- Muffin tins and liners
- Scissors
- Book (see Procedure section)

Procedure:

1. Have the children look at the pictures of bakers in *In the Night Kitchen* by Maurice Sendak (New York: Harper & Row, Pub., 1970).
2. Cut a band of white construction paper to fit around each child's head.
3. Have the children crumple tissue paper and help them puff it out, fold it over, and glue it along the inside of the band.
4. Staple the band together for a baker's hat.

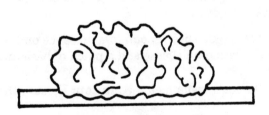

5. Explain to the children that bakers make breads, cakes, pies, cookies, doughnuts, and muffins.
6. Distribute the flour dough and cooking utensils to the children and give them plenty of time to be creative bakers.

Variation/Way to Extend:

- Have the children make the flour dough itself by mixing and kneading 1 cup flour, 1 cup salt, 2 tablespoons oil, and ½ cup water. Wrap it in plastic and store in the refrigerator.

I-171 MAKE A BOOK

Subject Area: Language Arts

Concepts/Skills: Enjoys looking at books
Develops a sense of touch
Uses short sentences to convey simple ideas

Objectives: The children will choose materials to use in the construction of individual books.

Materials:
- Oaktag cut into rectangles
- Notebook rings
- Hole puncher
- Construction paper
- Textured swatches
- Markers
- Fabric glue
- Several familiar books

Procedure:

1. Begin a discussion with the children about the library and about books. Use some familiar books to talk about the covers and pages.
2. Tell the children that they are each going to make their own books.
3. Distribute the precut rectangles to serve as front and back covers for each individual book.
4. Punch holes into the covers and pages made of construction paper.
5. Complete the books by using the notebook rings.
6. Make available to the children swatches of textured materials such as small pieces of cloth, carpeting, cotton, fur, ribbon, satin, sandpaper, velvet, and bark.
7. Let the children choose several (one for each page in their books) and use fabric glue to paste each piece of material in place.
8. Label each page or have the children describe what they feel about the page and write their words at the bottom of the page.

Variation/Way to Extend:

- Make a book with each child based on a particular area of interest. For example, cut out pictures from magazines that show children engaged in a park setting. Then highlight something different (a swing, ducks, benches, a drinking fountain, and so on) on each page. If you use a scene of a toy store, highlight each page with a toy that a two-year-old would enjoy, such as blocks, beads, dolls, teddy bears, and trucks.

I–172   MAKE-BELIEVE POST OFFICE

Subject Area: Social Studies

Concepts/Skills: Associates use with objects
Shows pleasure in dealing with people and things
Identifies picture of self from a snapshot

Objective: The children will become familiar with the materials used at the post office.

Materials: • Post office items
• Magnifying glass
• Large box

Procedure:

1. Prepare an examining box to encourage observation and exploration of related postal items.
2. Put a magnifying glass in the box along with postage stamps (cut off old envelopes), stamp pads, rubber stamps, stamp or sticker books, picture post cards, paper play money, old letters, cards, envelopes, divider (beverage carton), and a small scale.
3. Let the children play make-believe post office with these materials or just spend time exploring them.

Variation/Way to Extend:

• Take an instant photo of each child. Lay these out on a table and have each child find his or her own photo. Put each one in an envelope and demonstrate to the children how to write the name and address and to stamp them. Walk as a group to a mailbox and mail home these envelopes as presents to parents.

I-173 MERRY POSTAL WORKERS

Subject Area: Music

Concepts/Skills: Appreciates and participates in music
Performs with bells and rhythm instruments

Objectives: The children will learn a song about the mailman, play rhythm instruments to accompany it, and pretend to deliver mail.

Materials:
- Paper bag
- Fabric strips
- Stapler
- Rhythm instruments
- Record (see Procedure section)
- Record player
- Paper
- Pencils

Procedure:

1. Obtain a recording of "The Postman" by A. Diller and K. Page. Sheet music is available from Schirmer Music Publications, New York.
2. Fold a paper bag and attach fabric strips to form a shoulder bag.

3. Let the children scribble "notes" and "letters" to put in the bag and deliver to their friends in the room.
4. Have each child take a turn walking around the room, wearing the mailbag, and delivering the mail.
5. Play the recording during this time and have the other children play rhythm instruments to accompany the song.

Variation/Way to Extend:

- Use the rhythm sticks to practice playing loud and then soft, fast and then slow.

I-174 STORY TAPE

Subject Area: Creative Dramatics/Movement

Concepts/Skills: Develops listening and sequencing skills
Acts out a simple story

Objectives: The children will listen to a favorite taped library story book and then act out what they hear.

Materials:
- Tape recorder
- Tape
- Props to go along with book
- Favorite library book

Procedure:

1. Select a picture book from among the favorites enjoyed by your group of children. Choose the one they repeatedly ask to have read to them.
2. In preparation, tape-record yourself reading this story; read it slowly and use lots of expression. Then have the children listen to it once while they sit and enjoy it.
3. Next, give them some props and have them act out the story as it is being played on the tape. They can do this individually or in a small group.

Variation/Way to Extend:

- Make other audio tapes of picture book stories for your reading or listening corner. Ring a small bell to indicate when to turn the page so the children can follow along independently. Add poetry tapes and instrumental music tapes to your collection.

I–175   PRINT ART

Subject Area: Art

Concepts/Skills: Explores new materials
Develops fine motor movement of printing

Objectives: The children will create potato prints on a sheet of paper resembling a stamp.

Materials:
- Potatoes
- Knives
- Paper
- Containers
- Paper towels
- Pinking shears
- Tempera paint

Procedure:

1. Examine postage stamps this week and show the children where they are positioned on envelopes. Both the library and post office make use of rubber stamps, so a printing activity would be fun.
2. Make an ink pad from folded paper towels soaked with tempera paint and place in a flat container.
3. Cut potatoes to have basic shapes jutting out from an end.
4. Take pinking shears and trim the four edges of a large rectangular piece of paper to give it the look of a "stamp."
5. Have the children make potato-print pictures on the trimmed paper.

Variation/Way to Extend:

- For another printing experience, supply the children with cardboard tubes, empty thread spools, paper cups, egg carton sections, plastic forks, and so forth. Show them how to dip the objects in the paint pad and print on paper.

SUMMER

- ○ The Ocean, Rivers, and Lakes
- ○ Insects
- ○ Day and Night
- ○ Vacation and Travel

I-176   PLAYING IN THE OCEAN

Subject Area: Gross Motor Games

Concepts/Skills: Imitates actions
Jumps with two feet
Hops on one foot
Rolls a ball

Objective: The children will demonstrate gross motor movements.

Materials: • Beach balls
• Pictures of the ocean
• Open area outside
• Sandbox

Procedure:

1. Show the children pictures of the ocean. Ask, "Who has been to the beach?" "Did you like it?"
2. Take the children outside to the sandbox and let them play in the sand as if they were at the ocean.
3. Gather the children together and have them imitate you pretending to be at the ocean:

   Tip-toe to the edge of the water.
   Pretend the water is cold.
   Jump up and down in the water.
   Hop on one foot in the water.
   Pretend to swim in the water.
   Play catch with large beach balls.

Variations/Ways to Extend:

• Let the children build castles, pies, and so on in the sandbox. Be sure pails, shovels, and other sand toys are available for them to use.
• Have a water hose hooked up outside so the children can enjoy some supervised water play.
• Obtain an 11″ by 14″ art reproduction of *Children Playing at the Beach* (No. 2391) by Mary Cassatt from the National Gallery of Art, Publications Service, Washington, D.C. 20565. Write to the Gallery for current prices and any handling charges.

I-177 CIRCLES AND SQUARES

Subject Area: Math

Concept/Skill: Differentiates between a circle and a square

Objective: The children will be able to point to a circle and to a square upon request.

Materials:
- Pictures of beach scenes
- Beach materials
- Construction paper
- Glue
- Sand in a tall jar
- Beach tube

Procedure:

1. Show the children pictures of beach scenes, for example, the water, sand, and bathers.
2. Display items used at the beach, such as bathing suits, towels, pails, and goggles.
3. Let each of the children feel the sand in the jar.
4. Show the children a beach tube. Point out that it is in a shape of a circle. Let the children trace around the shape with their fingers.
5. Look around the room and ask the children to find other circles. Encourage them to make circles in the air with their arms.
6. Distribute the construction paper and assist each child in making circles of glue on the paper.
7. Sprinkle sand over the glued areas and shake off the excess.
8. Now follow the same procedure for squares. On a separate sheet of construction paper, draw squares with the glue and sprinkle with sand.
9. Find examples of squares in the room and let the children make squares in the air.
10. Ask the children to point to various squares and circles in the room as you call out the shapes.

Variation/Way to Extend:

- Draw circles and squares in the sandbox. Let the children count the number of shells as they place them inside the shapes.

I-178   THREE WISE MEN OF GOTHAM

Subject Area: Language Arts

Concepts/Skills: Repeats parts of a nursery rhyme
Counts to three

Objectives: The children will identify the ocean and waves and repeat parts of a nursery rhyme.

Material: • Book (see Procedure section)

Procedure:

1. Show a picture of the "Three Wise Men of Gotham" from a Mother Goose book of nursery rhymes, such as *The Mother Goose Treasury* by Raymond Briggs (New York: Dell, 1980) or *Mother Goose, the Old Nursery Rhymes* by Arthur Rackman (Long Island, NY: Sanford J. Durst, 1978, reprint of 1912 edition).

2. Show the children the ocean and the waves in the book. Ask, "Can you say 'ocean waves'?" Ask the children to count the men. "What town do we live in? These men live in a town named 'Gotham.'"

3. Read the nursery rhyme to the children:

   Three wise men of Gotham
   Went to sea in a bowl
   And if the bowl had been stronger
   My song would have been longer.

4. Ask the children to repeat each line after you.

Variation/Way to Extend:

• Give each child a large, flat cardboard box and have the children pretend they are sitting in a bowl, floating on the ocean. Repeat the rhyme to them as they pretend.

I-179 A FISHING WE WILL GO

Subject Area: Art

Concepts/Skills: Paints a big and a little object
Develops fine motor movements of painting and stringing

Objectives: The children will be able to paint the fish and distinguish big from little.

Materials:
- Pictures of fish and people fishing
- Precut big and little fish shapes
- Watercolor paints
- Paintbrushes
- Water
- String
- Hole puncher
- Plastic straws
- Stapler

Procedure:

1. Show the children pictures of fish that live in oceans, rivers, and lakes, as well as pictures of people fishing.
2. Precut two fish shapes, one big and one little, for each child.
3. Using waterpaints and brushes, have the children paint their own big and little fish.
4. When the fish are dry, punch a hole in each fish's mouth.
5. Guide the children in threading the string through the hole and stapling the string to the end of a plastic straw.

6. As they fish, sing along with the children "A-Fishing We Will Go" to the tune of "Farmer in the Dell."

Variations/Ways to Extend:

- Read *Big Ones, Little Ones* by Tana Hoban (New York: Greenwillow, 1976).
- Have the children listen to a recording of "Play of the Waves" (*La Mer* Suite) by Debussy from the *Adventures in Music* series. It is available from RCA Records, P.O. Box RCA 1000, Indianapolis, Ind. 46291.

I-180   WARM AND COLD

Subject Area: Science

Concept/Skill: Begins to understand hot and cold

Objective: The children will be able to identify hot and cold pans of water.

Materials:
- Two pans
- Water
- Ice cubes
- Pictures
- Water-play materials

Procedure:

1. Show the children pictures of oceans, rivers, and lakes. Emphasize the body of water with which children are most familiar. Also, discuss how many rivers and lakes are warmer in the summer and colder in the winter.

2. Demonstrate warm versus cold water temperatures by showing two pans of water, one *cold* (with ice) and the other *warm*. Allow the children to

   Feel the outside of both pans
   Feel the cold water and ice cubes
   Feel the warm water.

   Ask, "Which water would you rather take a bath in?"

3. Next, move the children to a water-play table for further experimentation with water (include plastic containers, funnels, sieves, plastic tubing, and brushes). Add warm water and then ice cubes. Discuss temperature changes.

Variation/Way to Extend:

- Have the children experience hot, warm, and cold objects, that is, cold juice; hot chocolate; hot water bottle; ice pack; and a heating pad, which gradually gets hot.

I-181   THIS LITTLE INSECT

Subject Area: Math

Concept/Skill: Becomes aware of more than two

Objective: The children will sing a counting song about insects.

Materials: • Picture
   • Words to verse (see Procedure section)

Procedure:

1. Borrow a large picture of an insect from the local library or find one in a children's magazine, such as *Ranger Rick's Nature Magazine* (National Wildlife Federation, 14-12 16th Street N.W., Washington, D.C. 20036). Make sure that the six insect legs are visible.

2. Point to each insect leg as the children say,

   One little, two little, three little legs,
   Four little, five little, six little legs,
   This little (*name of insect*) has six little legs,
   Six little legs has she.

3. Have the children repeat the song several times, each time assisting a new child in pointing to each leg as they are counted.

Variation/Way to Extend:

• Continue counting groups of six objects found in the classroom, for example, six toy cars, six dolls, and so forth.

I-182 LITTLE MISS MUFFET

Subject Area: Language Arts

Concepts/Skills: Describes what happened in two or three words
Repeats a nursery rhyme

Objectives: The children will be able to repeat a nursery rhyme and describe what happened to Miss Muffet.

Materials: • Book (see Procedure section)
• Small pillows
• Cottage cheese
• Cut-up fruit
• Small paper plates
• Spoons
• Soft, furry toy
• String

Procedure:

1. Show a picture of Little Miss Muffet from *The Mother Goose Treasury* by Raymond Briggs (New York: Dell, 1980). Read each line to the children:

   Little Miss Muffet
   Sat on a tuffet
   Eating some curds and whey;
   Along came a spider
   And sat down beside her
   And frightened Miss Muffet away.

2. Encourage the children to act out the rhyme. Do this by letting the children enjoy a snack of cottage cheese mixed with some cut-up fruit (for their "curds and whey") while they sit on small pillows. (*Tuffet* is a made-up word.)

3. Following the snack, tie a soft, furry toy to a piece of string and, while all the children repeat "Little Miss Muffet," move the toy near each child to "frighten" them away, laughingly, as a game.

4. Ask the children to tell you what happened to Miss Muffet.

Variation/Way to Extend:

• Provide an assortment of pipe cleaners in various sizes and colors. Ask the children if they would like to make pretend spiders and insects by twisting and shaping the pipe cleaners together. Use flour dough balls as the centers for the spider and insect bodies. (*Note:* Technically, a spider, which has eight legs, is not an insect but an arachnid.)

I-183   OBSERVING AN INSECT

Subject Area: Science

Concepts/Skills: Associates word with object
Identifies color

Objectives: The children will identify and observe a caterpillar and its movement.

Materials: • Caterpillar
• Jar
• Rubber band
• Nylon stocking or netting
• Leaf

Procedure:

1. Scoop up a caterpillar in a medium-sized jar and cover with a piece of nylon stocking or netting. Secure the material with a rubber band.
2. Show the jar to the children and ask: "What do you see?" "What color is it?" "How does it move?"
3. Remove the nylon covering, place a green leaf into the jar, and replace the nylon. Ask, "Do you think it will eat the leaf?" "What color is the leaf?" "Is it the same as the caterpillar?" "Should we let the caterpillar go back to its home?"

4. Take the children outdoors and free the caterpillar.
5. Allow the children to carefully watch as it crawls away.

Variation/Way to Extend:

• Return to the classroom and have the children try to move around the room like caterpillars.

I-184   GUESS THE INSECT

Subject Area: Creative Dramatics/Movement

Concepts/Skills: Recognizes various insects
Develops gross motor movements of hopping and crawling

Objective: The children will match the insect's name with its movement.

Materials: • Pictures of insects

Procedure:

1. Show the children pictures of insects, including a bee, a grasshopper, and an ant. (Borrow pictures of insects from the library or write to the National Audubon Society, Information Services Department, 950 Third Avenue, New York, N.Y. 10022, for their price list.)
2. Identify each picture for the children and demonstrate the movement of each insect. For example, buzz around the room with arms extended for a bee; hop around on two feet for a grasshopper; and crawl around on all fours for an ant.
3. Allow the children to demonstrate each insect and then play a game called "Guess the Insect." Call one child at a time off to the side of the room. Show the child one of the pictures and have the child move like that insect. Ask the other children if they know which insect is being acted out.

Variation/Way to Extend:

• Play a recording of "Dance of the Mosquito" by Laidov or "Flight of the Bumblebee" by Rimsky-Korsakov. Play the music during "Guess the Insect" or as background music at other times.

I-185   INSECT COLLAGE

Subject Area: Art

Concepts/Skills: Applies glue
Pastes pictures onto paper

Objectives: The children will be introduced to three insect pictures and create a collage of insects.

Materials: • Small magazine pictures of insects
• Construction paper
• Glue
• Marker

Procedure:

1. Allow the children time to examine small magazine pictures of three kinds of insects, such as bees, mosquitoes, and flies.
2. Identify the insects and discuss their similarities (all insects have six legs and two antennae).
3. Tell the children that they are each going to make a pretty picture by pasting these insects onto a sheet of paper.
4. Distribute the construction paper and glue and help each child paste the pictures onto his or her own paper.
5. Encourage the children to talk about where they would like to place each picture. Praise their efforts.
6. Write each child's name on his or her own collage and display all of them on a nearby wall or art area at the children's eye level.

Variations/Ways to Extend:

• Add materials to the collage, such as cotton, pieces of leaves, and twigs.
• Read the poem "Song of Summer" by Margaret W. Brown, found in her book *Nibble, Nibble* (Reading, Mass.: Addison-Wesley, 1959).

I-186   STAR CARD JUMP

Subject Area: Gross Motor Games

Concepts/Skills: Learns one-to-one correspondence
Indicates awareness of more than two
Jumps on two feet
Hops on one foot

Objectives: The children will identify the number of stars they see and jump or hop accordingly.

Materials: • Large cards with one, two, or three stars shown
• Large open area

Procedure:

1. Talk with the children about seeing stars in the sky at night.
2. Prepare large cards from oaktag that show either one, two, or three large "glittery" stars.

3. Show the children how to count "one star, two stars, three stars."
4. Tell the children to jump the number of times that a star appears on the card you hold up. For example, if you hold up the card with two stars, the children should jump two times.
5. After they have mastered doing this for up to three stars, have the children do the same thing by hopping on the left foot and then on the right.

Variation/Way to Extend:

• Have the children do the jumping and hopping in place or with a starting line and stopping line designated with masking tape on the floor.

I-187   HERE COMES THE SUN!

Subject Area: Art

Concepts/Skills: Paints with a large brush
Applies glue
Explores

Objectives: The children will construct, paint, and paste paper suns.

Materials:
- Paper plates
- Yellow paint
- Paintbrushes
- Paste
- Precut yellow strips of paper

Procedure:

1. Give each child a white paper plate to paint yellow like the sun.
2. Distribute the precut strips and talk about how they now have a circle and some straight lines.
3. Help them paste the lines around the edges of the plate to form a radiant sun.

Variation/Way to Extend:

- Talk about warm colors—how yellow, orange, and red are colors that make a person think about feeling warm. "What are some yellow, orange, and red things that are hot?" Also talk about cool colors—how green, blue, and purple are darker colors that make a person feel cool. "What are some cold things that are blue, purple, or green?"

Weekly Subtheme: Day and Night

I-188   TWINKLE, TWINKLE

Subject Area: Music

Concepts/Skills: Repeats parts of songs
Participates with pleasure

Objectives: The children will sing a traditional nursery song about stars.

Materials: • Words to "Twinkle, Twinkle, Little Star
• Pictures of a starry night

Procedure:

1. Teach the children the following song:

   Twinkle, twinkle, little star,
   How I wonder what you are.
   Up above the world so high,
   Like a diamond in the sky.
   Twinkle, twinkle, little star,
   How I wonder what you are.

2. Show the pictures of stars and talk with the children about nighttime and stars.

Variations/Ways to Extend:

• Listen to a recording of Mozart's *"Ah vous dirai-je, maman,"* which is a French song for piano that has the tune of "Twinkle, Twinkle Little Star."
• Read the Caldecott Honor book *A Child's Goodnight Book* by Margaret Wise Brown (Reading, Mass.: Addison-Wesley, 1943). You might also want to read her book *Goodnight Moon* (New York: Harper & Row, Pub., 1947).

I-189 SUMMER PARTY

Subject Area: Social Studies

Concepts/Skills: Gives first and last names when asked
Shows pleasure in dealing with other people and things

Objectives: The children will participate in a party for their parents and school personnel.

Materials:
- Food and beverages for party
- Paperware, glassware, flatware, and so forth
- Chairs, decorations, and so forth

Procedure:

1. As a culmination to the school year, plan a party or a picnic as a way to express farewells. This could be an ice cream social or an afternoon punch-and-cookie party. Let the children help decide.
2. Have the children help color invitations and mail them to their families and other guests. The entire school community can be invited—the pediatrician who serves as the school's doctor, van drivers, mail carriers, secretaries, and everyone else who performed important services for the children during the year.
3. Help the children mix juice, put ice cubes in pitchers, spread cheese on crackers, set up paper plates, decorate, and so on.
4. Encourage each child to give his or her first and last names as they meet other children's parents. You might say the names for the children and have them repeat their names when necessary.
5. A school newsletter with children's drawings and humorous quotes might be distributed to sum up some of the year's activities and children's accomplishments.

Variation/Way to Extend:

- Evaluate your program, materials, and equipment in terms of the uses of indoor and outdoor space, now that the longer days of summer are approaching. Many activities, such as manipulatives, dress up, and easel art, can be moved outside in the sunshine or under a shady tree. Try to secure a piece of outdoor furniture and put it under a tree to provide a pleasant place to look at a book, hear a story, or talk with a friend.

I-190   ALL IN A DAY

Subject Area: Language Arts

Concepts/Skills: Knows that different activities go on at different times of the day

Acts out a simple story

Objective: The children will demonstrate some activities as a description is read to them.

Material: • Book (see Procedure section)

Procedure:

1. Read *All Day Long* by Richard Scarry (New York: Western, 1976), which emphasizes a typical daily routine.
2. After reading the story once to the children, invite a few of them to act out some of the pages, such as when Bear gets out of bed, brushes his teeth, washes his face, combs his hair, gets dressed, makes his bed, and eats breakfast.
3. As you read, be sure the children hear the sequence of events and act them out accordingly.

Variation/Way to Extend:

• Read *The Summer Noisy Book* by Margaret W. Brown (New York: Harper & Row, Pub., 1976).

I-191   SUMMER PICNIC

Subject Area: Social Studies

Concepts/Skill: Shows pleasure in dealing with people and things

Objectives: The children will help prepare sandwiches and enjoy a summer picnic.

Materials:
- Bread
- Peanut butter
- Honey
- Fruit
- Plastic sandwich bags
- Plastic knives
- Milk
- Napkins
- Paper plates
- Picnic basket
- Blankets

Procedure:

1. Explain to the children that they will be going on a picnic, something that many people do during the summer and while on vacation.
2. Assist each child in making a peanut butter and honey sandwich.
3. Place the sandwiches, fruit, milk, and paper products in a picnic basket and take several blankets.
4. While walking to a picnic spot, take note of the warm weather and the sun (or clouds) and talk about summer.
5. Spread the blankets and assist the children in enjoying a picnic.

Variations/Ways to Extend:

- Give the children free play in the sandbox and wading pool. Provide them with pails, shovels, rakes, tubes, funnels, and sponge balls.
- Read *I'm the King of the Castle* by Shigeo Watanabe (New York: Putnam Publishing Group, 1982).

I-192   SEASHELL JEWELRY BOX

Subject Area: Math

Concepts/Skills: Counts to two
                     Indicates awareness of more than two

Objectives: The children will construct a jewelry box and decorate it by counting and pasting seashells onto it.

Materials: • Pictures
                 • Small seashells
                 • Glue
                 • Blue tissue paper cut in rectangles
                 • Small cardboard boxes

Procedure:

1. Show the children pictures of the ocean and beach vacation scenes.
2. Gather or buy small seashells. Explain how these came from the ocean and that people collect shells while visiting the beach.
3. Provide each child with a small jewelry-sized cardboard box.
4. Let each child glue the blue tissue rectangle to the box lid.
5. Encourage each child to count at least two (or more) shells to glue to the box.
6. These jewelry boxes can be brought home as gifts for family members.

Variations/Ways to Extend:

• Gather an assortment of different sized shells and have the children classify them as "big" or "little."
• Instead of using tissue paper, you might spray paint the box lids a light blue in advance of the lesson.

I-193 VACATION TOYS

Subject Area: Art

Concepts/Skills: Applies glue
Draws a horizontal line

Objective: The children will create a picture of toys used for summer play.

Materials:
- White drawing paper
- Pencils
- Crayons
- Precut shapes
- Glue

Procedure:

1. Give each child a piece of white paper. Assist the child in drawing a horizontal line across the middle of the paper.
2. With a green crayon, have the child color in the bottom half of the paper to represent grass. (For a beach scene, apply glue and sprinkle with sand. Then color the top half blue.)
3. Using glue and precut figures (or small pictures) resembling the shapes of summer toys (ball, pail, shovel, and wagon), have the children create a scene on the green (or sandy) part of the paper.

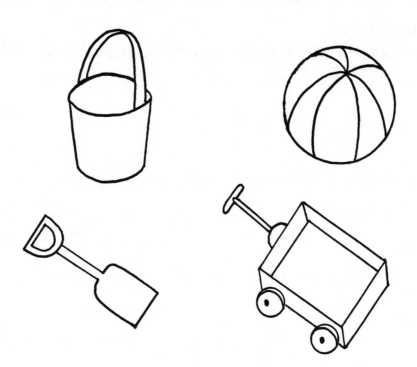

4. Above the line, let the child use a blue crayon to represent the sky.
5. Praise the children for their efforts and display the pictures on a wall at their eye level.

Variation/Way to Extend:

- Precut large circles and let the children paint these to resemble beach balls.

Weekly Subtheme: Vacation and Travel

I-194 JACK AND JILL

Subject Area: Language Arts

Concepts/Skills: Repeats part of a nursery rhyme
Begins to notice differences between safe and unsafe environments

Objective: The children will be more aware of the importance of safety during the summer.

Material: • Words to nursery rhyme (see Procedure section)

Procedure:

1. Tell the children you are going to read them a story about a little boy and a little girl who were on vacation with their parents. They went to get some water to water the plants around their vacation house, but on the way there was an accident.
2. Read the nursery rhyme "Jack and Jill." Tell the children that "fetch" means "to get" and "crown" is the top of your head.

   Jack and Jill went up the hill
   To fetch a pail of water.
   Jack fell down and broke his crown,
   And Jill came tumbling after.

3. Invite the children to repeat the poem.
4. Stress the importance of being careful while playing outdoors during the summer months.

Variation/Way to Extend:

• Have the children act out the nursery rhyme. Provide props for them.

Weekly Subtheme: Vacation and Travel

I-195   APPLE-BANANA COOLER

Subject Area: Nutrition/Foods Experience

Concepts/Skills: Lifts, drinks from, and replaces cup on the table

Objectives: The children will observe the creation of a nutritious summer cooler and then drink it without assistance.

Materials:
- Blender
- Paper cups
(for every four children)
- ½ cup yogurt
- ½ cup chilled apple juice
- 1 ripe banana
- Dash of cinnamon

Procedure:

1. Treat the children to a delicious summer or vacation drink called "Apple-Banana Cooler." Combine the ingredients in a blender and blend until well mixed.
2. Discuss the health benefits of eating good foods and drinks.
3. Serve the cooler to the children in paper cups.
4. Encourage them to lift the cups and drink by themselves.

Variation/Way to Extend:

- Explain to the children that apple juice comes from apples. Peel and slice several apples and serve as a snack. Let the children also watch an apple press (juicer) in action.

APPENDIX

SPECIAL SECTION
FOR PRESCHOOL DIRECTORS

Directors who use the *Preschool Curriculum Activities Library* will have a strong rationale to support their choices of topics and activities with children of different ages. Those who have implemented this curriculum can easily demonstrate how activities dealing with the same topic can be developmentally different and therefore appropriate for children who vary in age.

Directors are often asked by parents of home-bound children if activities are available from the school that the parent can use at home to teach the child. Again, the learning experiences in this book can be offered to parents to reduce fears about their children "missing" a preschool experience.

As parents become more sophisticated regarding their choice of a preschool, they may ask to see the curriculum. Parents can be shown how themes and topics incorporate many different skills and age-appropriate experiences. Such a rationale provides a clear understanding of the school's direction and creates a sense of integration and purpose for children, parents, and staff.

At its best, curriculum development is an ongoing process. Therefore, modify the themes and daily activities to meet the local and geographic needs of your children. The changes made, however, will be within a coherent framework so that each child, starting at age two, will be able to build upon the skills and knowledge earlier gained.

Described below are six steps to follow when creating or improving a preschool curriculum. It is suggested that a team of teachers address the questions following each step. New learning experiences can be created that complement and support the activities found in the *Library*, providing a well-rounded curriculum based on a planned approach.

Step 1: DETERMINE BELIEFS ABOUT HOW CHILDREN LEARN

According to Jones (1981), there are two basic approaches to creating curriculum for young children:

Approach 1—create activities based on children's interests
Approach 2—create activitites based on what children need to know

Proponents of Approach #1 believe that preschool children learn through direct experience, in their own creative ways, using real, natural objects. Preschoolers are in what Jean Piaget (1952) has called the "preoperational stage"; they thrive on free choice and manipulation of concrete objects in a stimulating environment. Also, Approach #1 advocates believe that abstract language in young children is largely undeveloped and therefore teachers should keep verbalizations such as questions and conveyance of facts to a minimum.

Proponents of Approach #2, however, argue that a curriculum based on concrete experiences, with a minimum of teacher "talk", is difficult to justify. Instead, it is felt that children must be prepared for living in an American culture which places much importance on verbal skill and high test scores. Approach #2, therefore, places emphasis on teacher conveyance of information and development of the children's ability to recall that information.

The curriculum presented in the *Library* offers a *combination* of both approaches. Learning experiences have been devised that are of high interest to children and encourage them to construct, move, and interact, while providing teachers with the opportunity to communicate information in an appropriate manner. It is clear that preschool children need direct, concrete, and high-interest experiences along with well-timed guidance and instruction. A combination of both approaches is essential to building an effective preschool curriculum.

Questions for Teachers
1. Which approach does your school follow?
2. Are there enough concrete experiences?
3. Is there opportunity for teacher conveyance of information?
4. What changes should be made?

Step 2: SELECT LONG-RANGE GOALS FOR THE CHILDREN

Four long-range early childhood goals are listed below. The activities described in the *Library* are based on these goals.

* Competence—to develop children's ability in the areas of language, numbers, and interest in books
* Cooperation—to enhance *self-concept* and *other-concept* through group activity and sharing experiences
* Autonomy—to encourage children to initiate, ask questions, and make limited choices
* Creativity—to construct new products, think of new ideas, and find alternative solutions

Questions for Teachers
1. Are the learning experiences you've created directed at achieving the four goals?
2. Is each goal approached through a variety of activities?

Step 3: ASSESS CHILDREN'S SKILLS-CONCEPTS NEEDS

The foundation of preschool curriculum planning is the observation and assessment of the individual needs of children. The Skills-Concepts Checklist found in this book can be duplicated, placed in each child's folder, and used to evaluate his or her progress during January and June of the school year. Anecdotal comments can be added to a child's folder to assist teachers in determining the skills that he or she has learned or that need to be strengthened.

Questions for Teachers
1. Do you take enough time to observe each child and record significant observations?
2. Do you keep a file folder on each child, containing the Checklist and anecdotal information?

3. Do you use your observations to make curricular changes?
4. How can the Checklist be modified to reflect special skills appropriate to your population of children?

Step 4: CREATE DEVELOPMENTALLY APPROPRIATE ACTIVITIES

All of the activities described in the *Library* are designed to achieve the long-range goals stated in Step 2 and develop the competencies found in the Skills-Concepts Checklist. Each learning experience develops one or more skills or concepts and is related to one of the six general content areas deemed appropriate for preschool children by Hildebrand (1980):

- The Child (personal data; health; body parts; relationship to family, school, and the world)
- The Community (people, workers, institutions, traditions)
- World of Plants (beauty, food)
- World of Machines (vehicles, small machines)
- World of Animals (pleasure, food)
- Physical Forces in World (weather)

Each activity in the *Library* is categorized into one of the following subject areas:

Language Arts	Art
Science	Music
Nutrition/Foods Experience	Math
Creative Dramatics/Movement	Thinking Games
Social Studies	Gross Motor Games

The children's learning can be further enhanced through additional field trips; the creation of learning experiences; and the use of traditional preschool materials and equipment such as blocks, sand, water, and paint (Seefeldt, 1980). The activities should be implemented in a classroom environment that, according to Harms and Clifford (1980), contains four characteristics:

- *Predictable* (well-defined activity centers, noisy and quiet areas, and labeled items)
- *Supportive* (child-sized equipment, play-alone space, and self-selection in activities)
- *Reflective* (children's artwork displayed, and multicultural and nonsexist materials)
- *Varied* (balance of active and quiet times, and indoor and outdoor play)

Questions for Teachers
1. Can the activities created and implemented by the staff be justified based on age-appropriateness?
2. How can the activities, themes, and subthemes found in this book be modified to fit the interests and needs of your children?
3. Are learning centers appropriately equipped?
4. Is the class environment predictable, supportive, reflective, and varied?

Step 5: PLAN FOR REPETITION OF CONCEPTS

Skills and concepts learned by young children need to be reinforced and extended. Many early childhood experts agree that facts must be placed into a structural pattern or frame of reference; otherwise, they will be forgotten. The pattern of activities found in this curriculum follows the model of primary and secondary reinforcement as described by Harlan (1980).

Harlan believes that concepts are built slowly from many simple facts or instances that can be generalized into a unifying idea. She recommends that teachers use her idea of *primary reinforcement* by creating a variety of activities (stories, fingerplays, songs, art, creative movement, math, food experiences, and so on) and by consciously reinforcing a concept or skill throughout each learning experience.

The curriculum presented here allows children to study one topic each week and be exposed to one of the ten subject areas (listed in Step 4) each day. By creating five different activities around one topic, the teacher has the opportunity to reinforce and extend concepts and skills.

Questions for Teachers

1. Are skills and concepts learned in one activity reinforced in other activities?
2. Can further activities be created that reinforce existing learning experiences?

Step 6: EVALUATE THE CHILDREN'S PROGRESS

Teachers can effectively evaluate the success of each activity by reviewing each lesson's stated behavioral objective and concepts/skills to be learned. They can then ask the question, "To what extent did each child learn what we intended to be learned?" Anecdotal notes can be briefly written and the Checklist can be used regarding each child's demonstrated behavior and skill acquisition. Decisions can be made providing for individual assistance or creating a new activity to reinforce a skill that a child may have had difficulty acquiring.

Questions for Teachers

1. When will the staff take some time (immediately after an activity, before lunch, after school) to evaluate what the children have learned?
2. What provisions can be made to assist children in acquiring certain skills?

REFERENCES

Harlan, Jean, *Science Experiences for the Early Childhood Years.* Columbus, Ohio: Chas. E. Merrill, 1980.

Harms, Thelma, and Richard M. Clifford, *Early Childhood Environmental Rating Scale.* New York Teacher's College Press, 1980.

Hildebrand, Verna, *Introduction to Early Childhood Education.* Columbus, Ohio: Chas. E. Merrill, 1980.

Jones, Edwin, *Dimensions of Teaching-Learning Environments: Handbook for Teachers.* Pasadena, Calif.: Pacific Oaks College Press, 1981.

Piaget, Jean, *The Origins of Intelligence in Children.* New York: International Universities Press, 1952.

Seefeldt, Carol, *Teaching Young Children.* Englewood Cliffs, N.J.: Prentice-Hall, 1980.

COMPLETE PRESCHOOL DEVELOPMENT PLAN

SKILLS-CONCEPTS CHECKLIST*
FOR TWO-YEAR-OLDS
(Developmental Characteristics)

A child who is 24 to 36 months of age tends to develop skills rapidly. The following abilities will emerge as the child approaches age three. The activities within this book have been designed to develop the skills and concepts listed below in a manner consistent with the child's needs and interests. Monitor the child's progress and evaluate it twice during the school year by placing a check (√) next to the skill or concept once it has been mastered.

Name _____ Birthdate _____

COGNITIVE

Personal Curiosity/Autonomy

	JAN.	JUNE
1. Shows curiosity and interest in surroundings		
2. Imitates the actions of adults		
3. Imitates play of other children		
4. Finds own play area or activity		
5. Enjoys looking at books		
6. Begins to notice differences between safe and unsafe environments (2½ to 3)		

Senses

7. Begins to develop senses of touch, smell, taste, and hearing		
8. Begins to place large puzzle pieces in appropriate slots		

Memory

9. Refers to self by name		
10. Points to common object on command		
11. Associates use with common objects		
12. Stacks three rings by size		
13. Knows that different activities go on at different times of the day (2½ to 3)		
14. Understands the idea of waiting for someone else to go first (2½ to 3)		

Creativity

15. Shows simple symbolic play (pretends block is a cup)		
16. Acts out a simple story (2½ to 3)		
17. Draws a face (no arms or legs) (2½ to 3)		

Comments:

_____

_____

_____

_____

* This Checklist was developed from the *Skill-Concept Development Checklists for Two Through Five Year Olds* (St. Louis County, Missouri: Parent-Child Early Education). Developed by the Ferguson-Florissant School District. Parts reprinted with their permission.

LANGUAGE

Sentence Structure	JAN.	JUNE
18. Describes what happened in two or three words		
19. Verbalizes wants ("Want water.")		
20. Repeats parts of songs, rhymes, and fingerplays		
21. Gives first and last names when asked (2½ to 3)		
22. Uses short sentences to convey simple ideas (2½ to 3)		

Listening

23. Listens to simple stories and songs		
24. Follows simple directions		
25. Places objects in, on, beside, or under		
26. Identifies loud and soft		

Labeling

27. Identifies own gender		
28. Identifies boy or girl		
29. Identifies self in mirror		
30. Names common objects in pictures		

Comments:

_____

_____

_____

_____

_____

SELF

31. Points to six body parts when named		
32. Puts on and removes coat unassisted		
33. Lifts and drinks from cup and replaces on table		
34. Spoon feeds without spilling		
35. Begins to understand cleanliness		
36. Helps put things away		

Comments:

_____

_____

_____

SOCIAL STUDIES

37. Identifies self from a snapshot		
38. Shows pleasure in dealing with people and things		
39. Values own property and names personal belongings (2½ to 3)		
40. Follows simple rules in a game run by an adult (2½ to 3)		

Comments:

_____

_____

_____

MATH

Counting	JAN.	JUNE
41. Understands the concept of "one"		
42. Counts two (repeats two digits)		
43. Indicates awareness of more than two (2½ to 3)		

Classifying

44. Groups things together by size (one category) (2½ to 3)		

Size Differences

45. Points to big and little objects (2½ to 3)		

Shapes

46. Differentiates circle and square (2½ to 3)		

Comments:

_____

_____

_____

SCIENCE (2½ to 3)

Concepts

47. Knows the names of three animals		
48. Can associate the words *grass, plants,* and *trees* with correct objects		
49. Identifies rain, clouds, and sun		
50. Begins to understand hard and soft		
51. Begins to understand hot and cold		
52. Begins to understand wet and dry		
53. Matches two color samples		

Comments:

_____

_____

_____

GROSS MOTOR

Arm-Eye Coordination

54. Throws a small object two feet		
55. Catches a rolled ball and rolls it forward		

Body Coordination

56. Jumps with two feet		
57. Claps with music		
58. Walks on tip toe		
59. Walks upstairs alone (both feet on each step) (2½ to 3)		
60. Walks downstairs alone (both feet on each step) (2½ to 3)		
61. Hops on one foot (2½ to 3)		

Comments:

_____

_____

_____

FINE MOTOR

Finger Strength and Dexterity	JAN.	JUNE
62. Fills and dumps containers with sand		
63. Turns single pages (2½ to 3)		

Eye-Hand Coordination		
64. Applies glue and pastes collage pieces		
65. Paints with a large brush		
66. Tears paper		
67. Strings five large beads		
68. Colors with a large crayon		
69. Rolls, pounds, and squeezes clay		
70. Draws a horizontal line		
71. Builds a six-block tower (2½ to 3)		
72. Uses scissors with one hand to cut paper (2½ to 3)		

Comments:

_____

_____

_____

_____

SKILLS-CONCEPTS CHECKLIST*
FOR THREE-YEAR-OLDS
(Developmental Characteristics)

A child who is 36 to 48 months of age continues to expand his or her cognitive, affective, and physical growth. The following abilities will emerge as the child approaches age four. The activities within this book have been designed to develop the skills and concepts listed below in a manner consistent with the child's needs and interests. Monitor the child's progress and evaluate it twice during the school year by placing a check (√) next to the skill or concept once it has been mastered.

Name _____ Birthdate _____

COGNITIVE

Personal Curiosity/Autonomy	JAN.	JUNE
1. Shows curiosity and the need to investigate/explore anything new		
2. Asks questions (Who?, What?, Where?, or Why?)		

Senses		
3. Demonstrates accurate sense of touch, smell, and taste		
4. Identifies common sounds		
5. Places objects on their outlines		
6. Observes objects closely		

Memory		
7. Recalls three objects that are visually presented		
8. Identifies what's missing from a picture		
9. Acts out simple everyday activities		

Logical Thinking		
10. Places three pictured events from a familiar story in sequence and expresses each picture sequence in three thoughts		

Relationships		
11. Pairs related objects and pictures, such as shoe and sock		
12. Recognizes which doesn't belong in a group of three items (for example, banana, chair, and apple)		

Creativity		
13. Draws a face with facial parts and stick arms and legs		
14. Dramatizes a simple story		
15. Uses animistic thinking (stuffed animals have human characteristics)		
16. Plays using symbols (objects stand for real objects)		

Comments: _____

_____

* This checklist was developed from the *Skill-Concept Development Checklists for Two Through Five Year Olds* (St. Louis County, Missouri: Parent–Child Early Education). Developed by the Ferguson–Florissant School District. Parts reprinted with their permission.

LANGUAGE

Sentence Structure

	JAN.	JUNE
17. Speaks in four- to six-word sentences		
18. Uses *I, you, me, he,* and *she* correctly		
19. Engages in simple conversation		
20. Memorizes and repeats simple rhymes, songs, or fingerplays of four lines		
21. Understands sentences and questions as indicated by a relevant response		
22. Names plural form to refer to more than one		
23. Describes action in pictures		

Listening

24. Listens to short stories and simple poems		
25. Follows two directions		
26. Understands opposites (up/down; open/closed; stop/go; happy/sad; fast/slow; hot/cold)		
27. Understands prepositions (in, out, over, under, on, off, top, bottom, in front of, in back of)		

Labeling

28. Names concrete objects in environment		
29. Recognizes and names articles of clothing worn		
30. Recognizes and names pieces of furniture		

Comments: _____

_____

_____

SELF

31. Points to and names body parts (head, hands, arms, knees, legs, chin, feet, and face parts)		
32. Tells own full name, sex, and age		
33. Feels good about self and abilities		

Comments: _____

_____

_____

SOCIAL STUDIES

Interpersonal

34. Enjoys being with other children		
35. Begins learning the give and take of play		
36. Begins participation in a group		

Concepts

37. Begins to understand that self and others change		
38. Understands that parental figures care for home and family		
39. Understands that people are alike and different in how they look and feel (3½ to 4)		

Comments: _____

_____

_____

MATH

	JAN.	JUNE
Counting		
40. Rote counts to ten		
41. Understands number concepts (when presented with a given number of objects, child can tell how many there are up to six)		
Classifying		
42. Sorts objects into two given categories (by size, shape, or color)		
Size Differences		
43. Understands concepts of full and empty		
44. Understands big/little; tall/short		
Shapes		
45. Points to and labels shapes		
46. Matches shapes (circle, square, triangle, and rectangle)		
Sets		
47. Matches sets containing up to five objects		
48. Constructs sets of blocks when given a model		

Comments:

_____

_____

_____

SCIENCE

	JAN.	JUNE
Concepts		
49. Understands that there are many kinds of animals		
50. Understands that animals move in different ways		
51. Understands that most plants make seeds for new plants		
52. Understands that seeds grow into plants with roots, stems, leaves, and flowers		
53. Understands that air is everywhere		
54. Understands that water has weight		
Colors		
55. Matches colors		
56. Points to appropriate color upon command		
57. Names three primary colors (red, yellow, and blue)		

Comments:

_____

_____

_____

GROSS MOTOR

Arm-Eye Coordination

	JAN.	JUNE
58. Catches a large ball from 5- to 8-foot distance		
59. Throws a ball overhand with accuracy from 4- to 6-foot distance		
60. Rolls a large ball to a target		
61. Throws a beanbag at a target five feet away		

Body Coordination	JAN	JUNE
62. Walks forward/backward on an 8-foot line		
63. Jumps three jumps with both feet		
64. Hops on one foot two or more times		
65. Moves body in response to simple teacher commands		
66. Walks on tiptoe		
67. Rides a tricycle		
68. Claps with music		

Comments: _____

_____

_____

_____

FINE MOTOR

Finger Strength and Dexterity

	JAN	JUNE
69. Makes balls and snakes with clay		
70. Pastes with index finger		

Eye-Hand Coordination

	JAN	JUNE
71. Strings at least four half-inch beads		
72. Puts pegs into pegboard		
73. Screws and unscrews nuts, bolts, and lids of various sizes		
74. Holds crayon with fingers rather than fist		
75. Paints with a large brush on large piece of paper		
76. Copies horizontal lines, vertical lines, circles, crosses, diagonal lines		
77. Uses scissors but does not necessarily follow lines		
78. Puts together a six- or seven-piece puzzle		
79. Laces following a sequence of holes		

Comments: _____

_____

_____

_____

SKILLS–CONCEPTS CHECKLIST*
FOR FOUR-YEAR-OLDS
(Developmental Characteristics)

A child who is 48 to 60 months of age typically demonstrates a large increase in vocabulary and physical abilities. The following abilities will emerge as the child approaches age five. The activities within this book have been designed to develop the skills and concepts listed below in a manner consistent with the child's needs and interests. Monitor the child's progress and evaluate it twice during the school year by placing a check (√) next to the skill or concept once it has been mastered.

Name _____ Birthdate _____

COGNITIVE

Personal Curiosity/Autonomy

	JAN.	JUNE
1. Shows an increasing curiosity and sense of adventure		
2. Asks an increasing number of questions		
3. Takes initiative in learning		
4. Shows an interest in the printed word		
5. Pays attention and concentrates on a task		

Senses

6. Demonstrates accurate sense of touch ("thick" or "thin") and smell		
7. Describes foods by taste (sweet, sour, and salty)		
8. Reproduces a simple pattern of different items from memory		
9. Ranks sounds (loud, louder, loudest; soft, softer, softest)		
10. Observes objects and pictures closely		

Memory

11. Recalls information previously taught		

Logical Thinking

12. Interprets the main idea of a story		
13. Orders pictures by time sequence to tell a story		

Relationships

14. Makes a simple comparison of two objects in terms of difference ("How are a cat and dog different?") and sameness ("How are a cat and dog alike?")		
15. Completes a statement of parallel relationships		

Predicting

16. Predicts what will happen next in a story or situation		
17. Predicts realistic outcomes of events ("What will happen if we go on a picnic?")		

* This checklist was developed from the *Skill–Concept Development Checklists for Two Through Five Year Olds* (St. Louis County, Missouri: Parent–Child Early Education). Developed by the Ferguson–Florissant School District. Parts reprinted with their permission.

Creativity	JAN.	JUNE
18. Responds well to nondirective questions ("How many ways can you think of to move across the room?")		
19. Proposes alternative ways of doing art experiences, movement activities, and story endings		
20. Represents thoughts in pictures		
21. Draws a human figure with major body parts		
22. Participates verbally or nonverbally in imaginative play or puppetry (socio-dramatic play)		
23. Acts out a familiar story or nursery rhyme as the teacher recites		

Comments: _____

_____

_____

LANGUAGE

Sentence Structure

	JAN.	JUNE
24. Speaks in six, eight, ten, or more words		
25. Makes relevant verbal contributions in small group discussion		
26. Shows understanding of past, present, and future tenses by using proper verb form		
27. Verbalizes songs and fingerplays		
28. Dictates own experience stories		
29. Describes a simple object using color, size, shape, composition, and use		
30. Describes a picture with three statements		

Listening

	JAN.	JUNE
31. Listens to directions for games and activities		
32. Listens to stories of at least ten minutes in length		
33. Retells five-sentence short story in sequence using own words		
34. Understands prepositions		

Labeling

	JAN.	JUNE
35. Labels common everyday items such as clothing, animals, and furniture		
36. Orally labels pictures and drawings ("That's a dog.")		

Letter/Word Recognition

	JAN.	JUNE
37. Verbally identifies letters in first name (and subsequently in last name)		
38. Identifies many letters of the alphabet		
39. Distinguishes words that begin with the same sound (*book/boy*)		
40. Names two words that rhyme in a group of three (*tie, road, pie*)		
41. Supplies a rhyming word to rhyme with a word given by the teacher		
42. Associates a letter with its sound in spoken words		

Comments: _____

_____

_____

_____

SELF	JAN.	JUNE
43. Touches, names, and tells function of parts of the body (head, eyes, hands, arms, feet, legs, nose, mouth, ears, neck, trunk, ankle, knee, shoulder, wrist, elbow, and heel)		
44. Verbalizes full name, address, age, birthday, and telephone number		
45. Identifies expressions of feelings		
46. Feels good about self and abilities		

Comments: _____

_____

_____

SOCIAL STUDIES

Interpersonal

47. Shows empathy toward other children		
48. Works cooperatively with adults		
49. Works and plays cooperatively with other children		

Concepts

50. Begins to understand that problems can be solved by talking and not fighting		
51. Understands that we wear appropriate clothing to protect us from extremes of weather		
52. Understands that families share responsibilities of work and recreation		

Comments: _____

_____

_____

_____

MATH

Counting

54. Counts from 1 to _____		
55. Understands ordinal positions first through fifth		
56. Recognizes and orders the cardinal numerals in sequence		
57. Solves simple verbal problems using numerals ("If you have two pieces of candy and I give you one more, how many will you have?")		

Classifying

58. Classifies objects by color, size, shape, and texture		

Size Differences

59. Orders and compares size differences (big, bigger, biggest; small, smaller, smallest; short, shorter, shortest; long, longer, longest)		

Shapes

60. Points to and names: triangle, circle, square, rectangle, and diamond		

Quantitative Concepts

	JAN.	JUNE
61. Distinguishes between concepts of "some," "most," and "all"		
62. Compares objects as to weight ("Which is heavier?" "Which is lighter?")		
63. Understands concepts of "full," "half full," and "empty"		
64. Understands fractions (½, ¼, whole)		

Sets

65. Identifies a set as a collection of objects having a common property		
66. Establishes a one-to-one correspondence through matching members of equivalent sets (matching six cowboys to six cowboy hats)		
67. Distinguishes between equivalent and non-equivalent sets through matching		
68. Understands that each number is one more than the preceding number ("What is one more than two?")		
69. Identifies an empty set as one having no members		

Comments:

_____

_____

_____

SCIENCE

Concepts

70. Understands that each animal needs its own kind of food and shelter		
71. Understands that plants need water, light, warmth, and air to live		
72. Understands that many foods we eat come from seeds and plants		
73. Understands that some things float in water and some things sink in water		
74. Understands the balance of nature—that is, animals need to eat plants, vegetables, and insects in order to live		
75. Understands that plant life, animal life, and other aspects of the environment must be respected		

Colors

76. Points to and names colors		

Comments:

_____

_____

_____

GROSS MOTOR

Arm–Eye Coordination

77. Catches a ball away from body with hands only (large ball/small ball)		
78. Throws a ball or beanbag with direction		
79. Throws a ball into the air and catches it by self		
80. Bounces and catches a ball		

	JAN.	JUNE
Body Coordination		
81. Walks forward and backward on a line ten feet long without stepping off		
82. Walks a line heel-to-toe eight feet long without stepping off		
83. Balances on foot for five seconds		
84. Stops movement activity upon teacher's direction		
85. Moves body creatively upon teacher's direction		
86. Claps with music		

Rhythm

	JAN.	JUNE
87. Claps and marches in time with music		
88. Responds to rhythms with appropriate body movements		

General Movement

	JAN.	JUNE
89. Produces the following motions: walks backwards, runs smoothly, marches, skips, gallops, hops four times on each foot, walks heel-to-toe, and walks and runs on tiptoe		

<u>Comments:</u> _____

_____

_____

_____

FINE MOTOR

Finger Strength and Dexterity

	JAN.	JUNE
90. Folds and creases paper two times		
91. Folds paper into halves, quarters, and diagonals		

Eye-Hand Coordination

	JAN.	JUNE
92. Strings ten small beads		
93. Follows a sequence of holes when lacing		
94. Works a puzzle of ten or more pieces		
95. Uses crayon or pencil with control within a defined area		
96. Connects a dotted outline to make a shape		
97. Follows a series of dot-to-dot numerals, 1–10, to form an object		
98. Reproduces shapes (circle, square, triangle, and rectangle)		
99. Controls brush and paint		
100. Uses scissors with control to cut along a straight line and a curved line		

<u>Comments:</u> _____

_____

_____

_____